ESCAPE TO FREEDOM

ESCAPE TO FREEDOM

by

TONY JOHNSON

LEO COOPER

First published in Great Britain in 2002 by
LEO COOPER
an imprint of Pen & Swords Books
47 Church Street, Barnsley
South Yorkshire S70 2AS

Copyright © Tony Johnson 2002

ISBN 0 85052 894 1

A CIP record for this book is
available from the British Library

Typeset in 11/13pt Sabon by
Phoenix Typesetting, Ilkley, West Yorkshire

Printed in England by CPI UK

To Joyce
Who waited

Contents

ACKNOWLEDGEMENTS

The task of accurately describing events that occurred more than half a century ago would have been a most daunting exercise were it not for the invaluable assistance provided by many friends and acquaintances, who were able to refresh and supplement a memory dimmed by the passage of time. I am most grateful to them all.

I owe a special thanks to the surviving members of my crew; Geoffrey Hall, Albert Symonds and William Ostaficiuk and my Squadron Commander, Group Captain Dudley Burnside DSO, OBE DFC and Bar (RAF Rtd.) for their most helpful information and advice. Also to my wife Joyce, for her encouragement – and infinite patience.

The Crown Copyright material for this work is reproduced with the kind permission of the Controller of Her Majesty's Stationery Office.

FOREWORD

by

Group Captain Dudley Burnside DSO OBE DFC (RAF Rtd),
wartime Officer Commanding 427 and
195 Squadrons, Bomber Command.

It was indeed a great privilege to lead a squadron in Bomber Command in 1942–43 and again in 1944–45 and to share the appalling dangers of continuous raids over Germany with that magnificent band of young aircrews whose devotion to duty and outstanding courage are legion and of which the author of this book was a typical example.

As his Commander-in-Chief, Marshal of the Royal Air Force, Sir Arthur Harris, put it 'these young men carried unceasing war to the enemy against fearful odds for over five years, and for much of that time alone whilst we lacked the means for any other attack'.

I know only too well the experience of being coned by searchlights, of being attacked by nightfighters and blasted by flak. But to read such a first-hand account of the terrifying moments immediately following a fatal direct hit, of the aircraft turning upside down before spiralling vertically to earth is not only to bring sharply into focus the incredible luck of those of us who survived one or more tours of operations physically unscathed but to pay the greatest tribute and admiration to those such as Tony Johnson who, having miraculously baled out of his doomed Wellington aircraft, continued to display incredible courage and endurance in very hostile enemy territory.

His description of life as a prisoner of war and his extraordinary adventures during his two escapes will surely serve to remind future generations of the unsurpassed devotion to duty and heroism of wartime aircrews against great odds both in the air and on the ground.

Dudley Burnside
Windsor

Chapter 1

Nasty Prang

The unmistakable drone of aircraft engines being run up to operating temperature reverberated through the North Yorkshire countryside in which the farming village of Dalton-on-Tees nestled. The now familiar sound of squadron activity at RAF Croft airfield, situated to the west of the village, was the cue for the local 'fan club' of civilians and servicemen patronizing the busy Crown and Anchor public house, to take their drinks out into the fresh air to watch the aircraft take-off. Some would watch in silence while others would wave frantically as the aircraft roared over the perimeter security fence, some alarmingly low as they lifted into the beautiful April sky. However, there were also those who worked the farms skirting the airfield, and many light sleepers who cursed the day when the Ministry of Defence compulsorily purchased the land to build an airfield which was completed in 1941 for Bomber Command. Despite the fact, apart from most Sundays, there was little or no noise abatement practised on the airfield around bedtime and before noon when the aircraft were air tested, these folk were very much aware that there was a war on and had taken the personnel serving at the bustling RAF Station on their doorstep.

It was late evening on 6 April 1943, and RAF Croft was the base for 427 (Lion) Squadron of the Royal Canadian Air Force. The Squadron was one of nine in the recently formed 6 Group RCAF, a group that became operational on 1 January 1943 and was equipped with Vickers Wellington Mk III and Mk X medium bombers.

I was a crew member of one of four Wellington aircraft leaving their dispersal pans and being taxied around the perimeter track to take up the second position in a queue at the end of the runway to wait for its turn to take-off. The four aircraft were about to carry out a night exercise by the codename 'Bullseye' which, in effect, was to simulate a raid on London to give our nightfighter pilots experience at homing in on hostile bombers. More importantly, it was good experience for us rookie crews who had little operational experience over enemy territory: particularly if we lost our bearings in cloud and flew into a barrage of balloons over Leeds, Sheffield or London itself. Quite exciting, really.

Soon the Airfield Controller in his chequered van gave the green light for us to take-off. As the German Luftwaffe monitored our radio frequencies, strict radio silence was observed by Bomber Command operators during aircraft movements to carry out air tests, training or operations against the enemy. The maintenance of radio silence denied the Luftwaffe the means of assessing our strength, the likely flight path of the bomber force, and thus lessened the odds of Luftwaffe nightfighters waiting in ambush to tenaciously defend their Fatherland. That is why the NCO in the chequered van relied upon the Aldis lamp rather than communicate with the pilots on shortwave radio.

Steve, my skipper, released the brakes and eased the throttles forward and the aircraft gathered speed along the runway in the evening dusk. From my position with my head in the astrodome – a perspex bubble on top of the fuselage – I had an excellent view through 360 degrees. We slowly passed a group of spectators waving us off near the van, gradually increasing speed along the 2,000 yards of reinforced concrete runway. On reaching flying speed we lifted off with plenty of runway to spare, to start to climb after the aircraft that had preceded us on take-off less than a minute before. Once off the ground and without the burden of a bomb load – we were not really about to bomb London – we climbed fairly rapidly as we circled the airfield to wait to be joined by the remaining two aircraft before setting course.

Standing at the astrodome I had a panoramic view of the airfield as we climbed away from it. I was also able to watch the next

Wellington as it took off, and the last aircraft turning onto the runway for its turn to take to the air. As the aircraft following immediately after us left the runway it climbed no more than fifty feet when, suddenly, its port wing dipped as it banked, obviously out of control, and headed in a shallow glide towards the front door of the East Vince Moor farmhouse in the occupation of farmer Pearson and his family. Some seventy feet before it reached the farmhouse, the doomed aircraft was brought to an abrupt halt by a clump of aged elm trees, and disintegrated on impact. Flying debris showered the surrounding area as, in a few breathtaking seconds, the twisted wreck of the aircraft erupted into a blazing inferno as some 700 gallons of high octane aviation fuel ignited, sending a huge fireball into the evening air. I knew that the intense heat would rapidly fuse the light airframe alloys and incinerate those of the five man crew trapped in the instant crematorium who, mercifully, had either been killed outright or knocked unconscious by the terrific force of impact. It seemed incredible to me that in a matter of seconds, on such a pleasant evening, men would die in what was considered an airworthy and air tested aircraft.

Although I was stunned by what I had seen, I started shouting to the rest of the crew to let them know what had happened to one of our flight. By the time I had realized that it would be an advantage to switch on the mouthpiece of my intercom, I found that the other crew members had been informed of the prang by Bill, the rear-gunner, who had also had a good view of the action taking place at East Vince Moor farm. Steve, our pilot, responded to our suggestion that we fly over the scene of the crash to obtain a closer look. In horror we looked down into the dense, billowing plume of black oily smoke rising from what, a few moments before, had been a twenty ton aircraft with its crew complement of five young men.

Station fire tenders, water bowsers, ambulances and other rescue services, accompanied by station personnel on foot or cycle, could be seen stampeding across the airfield to converge on the crash site.

One of the Pearson family, the farmer's son, had witnessed the

3

crash from the Crown and Anchor public house and, with friends, raced to the farmhouse believing the worst had happened, but fortunately the elm trees had protected the family from certain disaster. Had Wellington X HE743 been carrying its operational load of nine 500 lb bombs, then there would have undoubtedly been a far greater loss of life at East Vince Moor farm that night.

Our rear-gunner considered that 'it was a bloody nasty prang' and we all wondered which crew had 'bought it' this time. After flying over the scene we climbed and set course for London, to concentrate on the task in hand and try to forget the tragic event we had just witnessed.

As only two of the four aircraft carrying out the 'Bullseye' had successfully taken off, the pilot of the last aircraft who, having witnessed first hand the result of engine failure, decided that he was far too traumatized to continue the exercise, taxied his aircraft back to its dispersal pan, parked it, cut the engines and, so far as the night's exercise was concerned, called it a night. With so much activity going on across the airfield, he could not have taken off in any event.

• Witnessing the stricken aircraft crash and burn, and being aware that a number of our mess mates had perished in the inferno, really had an adverse effect on our morale. I harboured many fears, the greatest being to be trapped fully conscious in a blazing aircraft – Wellington aircraft did tend to catch fire quickly when they crashed. Whatever our fears, we did our best not to show them and to carry on as normal.

As we flew south each member of the crew settled down to his particular skills. The pilot and the navigator were kept the busiest, while the bomb-aimer and rear-gunner had little to do but stare out into the night, straining their eyes to spot other aircraft, whether friend or foe, and to watch out for the silver barrage balloons drifting at the end of their steel hawsers over cities straddling our course to London. Leeds, Sheffield, Leicester and Northampton could become major hazards should we be flying too low an altitude and stray off course. It is an unfortunate fact that rookie crews are prone to errors which invariably prove fatal, and I wanted so much to survive the war and, perhaps

4

become a veteran wireless operator. Already the events of the evening had made me wonder why I volunteered for such an insecure wartime job as aircrew.

Geoff spent most of his time crouched over his dimly lit desk checking and rechecking the coordinates to satisfy himself that the aircraft was on track to London. He had the benefit of a comparatively new navigation aid, the TR 1335 'GEE', which by a process of measuring the time lag between impulses, or blips, appearing on a small green round screen from three separate transmitters, Geoff was able to plot the right course for the pilot to steer. With its introduction to Bomber Command in 1942 greater accuracy was achieved in finding a target. It did away with dead reckoning and astro navigation. Already the German Luftwaffe had perfected a means of jamming 'GEE' under certain circumstances and, like most sensitive equipment, it often became unserviceable after being subjected to hours of continual vibration, and our Wimpy – Wellington – certainly vibrated and lurched from air pocket to air pocket. When 'GEE' did fail, then it was back to the old and proven methods of navigation and, on the few occasions when the stars could not be seen, the rest of the crew would rely on me to obtain radio magnetic bearings to verify a course and steady nerves.

I would maintain a listening out watch on my receiver just in case we were recalled. The morse code was used in all air to ground communications, except that the pilot had an air to ground radio with a very limited range which he could use to obtain landing permission in extreme emergencies. Then there was our intercom earphones and mouthpiece cleverly incorporated into our flying helmets with which, provided the dangling socket was plugged in, we talked to one another – but only if absolutely necessary. In the event of being attacked by a fighter aircraft – whether friend or foe – I would figuratively speaking, don my air-gunner's cap and scramble into the front turret to man the two .303 Browning machine guns.

Bert, the bomb-aimer, would normally occupy the seat beside the pilot until the target area was reached. He would then get down into the nose of the aircraft to lie behind the bombsight. He was also qualified to take over the controls and fly the aircraft should the pilot need a break, be seriously wounded or killed in action. To break the monotony of staring into space, Albert would take up his position at his bombsight to 'blitz' any city en route that took his fancy – all part of a vigorous RAF training programme.

Isolated in the tail end turret, Bill would try to maintain a comfortable body temperature by operating the hydraulics to elevate and depress the four Browning machine guns and to swivel the turret from side to side through 180 degrees, not only to search the sky but to prevent the hydraulics from freezing up. Although he was the only crew member issued with an electrically heated flying suit, this did not make him feel cosy and warm. He was always bemoaning the fact that he was at the wrong end of the aircraft. He walked into a Calgary, Canada, recruiting office and offered his services as pilot but had to settle for the trade of air-gunner. But then, all aircrew volunteered to be pilots.

As it transpired all three aircraft taking part in the exercise were recalled to base less than an hour after taking off. In view of the earlier events of the evening, we were thankful to be able to land and park the aircraft without any further vexations of the spirit. As it was now quite dark we were unable to see what was going on at the crash site, except that there was some subdued lighting there. Our ground crew were waiting as we taxied onto the dispersal pan. Collecting together our parachutes, charts, logs and other necessary paraphernalia, we dropped one by one to the ground through the main hatch in the nose of the aircraft. Then hastily unbuckling our parachute harnesses we stood in a line at the edge of the pan and watered the buttercups and daisies – a necessary ritual performed by 'bomber boys' after every trip.

The performance required to adjust or remove a flying suit and parachute harness, coupled with the frustrating and impossible task of aiming and successfully hitting the Elsen toilet pan in a vibrating and lurching aircraft, made it desirable to hold out if only to enjoy the sheer relief of peeing on the greensward.

We learned from the ground crew that the pilot and wireless operator had been killed in the crash, the other three crew members had been thrown clear on impact but were very seriously injured. The pilot, Sergeant A. C. Ash, was a Canadian, while his wireless operator was Sergeant J. K. Dodds from just over the border in County Durham. It had already been concluded by the ground crew that Sergeant Ash and his crew had been the victims of an engine failure just after becoming airborne; the sudden loss of power at a critical stage of take-off inevitably resulted in the aircraft banking as it fell out of the sky and crashing before the pilot was able to regain control; one of a pilot's worst nightmares. The alternatives of structural failure or pilot error could not be ruled out but were dismissed as unlikely under the circumstances. Tuesday, 6 April 1943, had turned out to be a very sad day with the loss of Wellington X HE473, squadron markings ZL-X, and Sergeants Ash and Dodds – who would soon become official statistics, and remembered only by their loved ones and friends.

We were soon picked up by the crew wagon and conveyed nearly a mile to the Safety Equipment Section, where we disposed of our parachutes and Mae Wests – inflatable life jackets. On this occasion there was none of the friendly banter with the duty WAAF parachute packers, a tacit form of respect for the dead. Normally we would have friendly and affectionate repartee with the girls, always with the greatest respect as our lives could well depend on their skills in servicing our parachutes and dinghies.

Next it was over to the Crew Room to stow our flying gear in the lockers – except our lambs wool lined flying boots. This comfortable footwear was adopted for everyday use within the precincts of the airfield and The Chequers public house. After reporting to our respective section officers, in my case the Signals Officer, for a quick debriefing, we made our way to the Sergeants' Mess for something to drink and eat. The hot cocoa and sandwiches left out for us in the cookhouse were invariably given a miss for a number of reasons, the main one being that the food was anything but appetizing.

The nasty 'prang' in which two of our 'bods' had 'bought it' was the sole topic of conversation, mainly because it had happened on our own doorstep rather than somewhere on enemy territory during a raid, when the only evidence of anything untoward happening were the empty spaces in the mess the following morning and aircraft missing from their parking places. The blame, as always, was placed squarely upon the scourge of the RAF in general and aircrew in particular – the Gremlins. Infinitely more cunning and mischievious than leprechauns, gremlins were responsible for all the unexplained mishaps that occurred on the ground, but more so in the air. Sightings of these little buggers were extremely rare and, apart from one exception to my knowledge, seemed only to be spotted by airmen well under the influence of alcohol. A fellow student on my wireless course at No. 2 Signals School at RAF Yatesbury in Wiltshire saw several gremlins. He went to some lengths to convince the instructor and classmates that he could observe gremlins balancing along the conduits housing the telegraphy circuitry coupling the instructor to each student and that they were interfering with his morse reception and transmission. The instructor quickly formed the opinion that the effort required to absorb the incessant dot dash characteristics of the code tapped out at approximately twenty words per minute had finally driven the poor soul 'round the bend'. He was taken off the course immediately and packed off to a psychiatric clinic before he could 'contaminate' the whole course.

As other crews began to arrive in the mess, it began to liven up. Already the resident pianist, a veteran on the squadron with many trips over enemy territory, was surrounded by beer swigging airmen of the 'Lion Choral Society', to which all paid up members of the mess were affiliated. A popular ballad with the singers was the lyrical rendering of 'Here's to the dead already, and here's to the next man to die' repeated after quaffing from their beer glasses. Another favourite was sung to the music of the Australian 'Waltzing Matilda' which went something like, 'Ops in a Wimpy, ops in a Wimpy, who'll come on ops in a Wimpy with me? The rear-gunner sang as he reached for his parachute, who'll come on ops in a Wimpy with me?'. They were repeated again and again as the evening wore on. The billiards table at the other end of the mess was surrounded by a 'school' of airmen noisily engaged in the game of craps. Believed to be of North American origin, and popular with the Canadians, it is a game in which fortunes were won or lost at the throw of a pair of dice. It was a fascinating game to watch. After bets were placed, the person holding the dice in one of his clenched fists would proceed to talk to them most enthusiastically and advisedly to land on the table to his financial advantage. The dice would then be lobbed onto the table with, perhaps, a shout of 'be good to me you little darlings, a seven or eleven!' The dice would be lobbed onto the table for as many times as it was required for a winning or losing combination of spots to appear. A 'lucky' craps player could win hundreds of pounds on or soon after a pay day, but could also be killed a few hours later on a bombing raid. The fact that craps was the most popular gambling game in the mess was evident by the many cigarette burn marks on the green baize and polished wood surround of the billiards table – much to the annoyance of those who preferred to play billiards or snooker.

While the Canadians introduced us to craps, poker, pool, peanut butter and maple syrup, they also showed remarkable enthusiasm for the English pub favourites of darts, dominoes, brag and pontoon. They also relished fish and chips, sausages and mash, and the beverages of Burton, Youngers and Newcastle brown ale. Some, of course, preferred whisky until funds ran low. The Canadian brands of Sweet Caporal and McDonald cigarettes, although milder, were soon favoured because they could be purchased cheaper than Wills and Players brands.

The Canadians were generally a happy-go-lucky bunch of characters who were easy to get along with. There were occasions when they were inclined to be unnecessarily reckless, and seemed to lack the strict discipline instilled in RAF recruits during training. Nevertheless, they were patriotic, courageous, over-sexed, but dedicated to the cause of fighting the Axis powers. The French Canadians, who came mainly from Quebec and Montreal, integrated well into squadron life despite the language difficulty. All in all, there was a good Commonwealth mix at Croft, a mix that could be found on any of the squadrons that made up 6 Group, although they were still a long way from becoming fully Canadianized.

This party type atmosphere in the mess typified aircrew behaviour when on stand-down from operational sorties, or following a crash like the one at Vince Moor Farm. It belied their true feelings. It was always a setback to morale to learn of comrades missing or killed on operations, although there was always a glimmer of hope that those missing would either evade capture and get back to the squadron or become prisoners of war. To have a fatal crash on home ground, as it were, was an entirely different matter; a much more personal thing that made it difficult not to become emotionally involved. I had known Sergeant Dodds for some months, as we had been on an Operational Training Unit together before meeting at Croft.

Finishing our drinks, we made our way to our Nissen hut which was one of a colony tucked away in a thicket at the edge of the airfield, conveniently near the cookhouse and the main gate. All was quiet and peaceful as we made our way along the narrow pathways leading to the Nissen huts. The landing lights had been extinguished, but there was still some activity at East Vince Moor farm. Along with the others that skirted the airfield, this farm had been the subject of a compulsory purchase of hundreds of acres of its fertile land. Soon after the outbreak of war the Ministry of Defence bought up approximately 5,000 acres of land to the west of the villages of Croft and Dalton-on-Tees to provide a satellite airfield for RAF Middleton St George (now Teesside Airport), which was four miles to the east of Croft in the County of Durham – the most northerly Bomber Command operational airfield in England. Construction of the airfield, which is situated south of the River Tees and to the west side of the A167 Darlington–Northallerton road, was completed in 1941. It was initially occupied by 78 Squadron, then in 4 Group, and equipped with Armstrong-Whitworth Whitley medium bombers. The airfield became the base for 427 (Lion) Squadron RCAF on 1 January 1943.

Croft is 180 feet above sea level and its airfield the highest in 6 Group. The standing joke was that our squadron had the edge on more southerly squadrons who had to climb more from take-off to gain the predetermined cruising height. For most targets in enemy territory we had the furthest distance to travel, although this extra mileage was mostly flown over the North Sea. The airfield main runway was 2,000 feet in length and laid in an east–west direction. There were also two 1,400 feet lengths of secondary runways which formed the familiar triangle when viewed from above. A large maintenance hanger dominated the area in which were the administration and other buildings necessary for the efficient functioning of an operational Bomber Command station.

*　　*　　*

I answered the call to arms in January 1941. Although not quite eighteen years of age the RAF recruiting officer made no request to see my birth certificate and, after giving me a short test, informed me that I would be required to attend an Aircrew Selection Board. Within a few days I attended RAF Uxbridge, but was unable to persuade the panel of officers that an elementary education was a prerequisite to becoming an ace pilot. I passed the medical examination with 'flying colours' and as there were other aircrew categories to be filled, I readily accepted the offer to train as a wireless operator/air gunner as a consolation.

I was sworn in on 13 January 1941, and then followed two years of alternating between ground duties and the wireless courses at Blackpool, RAF Yatesbury and RAF Compton Basset, and the gunnery course at 1 Gunnery School, RAF Pembrey in South Wales. It was a great moment for me to throw away the white aircrew cadet flash worn on my forage cap and sew on the sergeant's chevrons and aircrew trade insignia. I was as pleased as punch, but nevertheless felt some sadness for those who had failed to make the grade on the way – or had been freaked out by gremlins.

Following a period of leave, I was posted to 22 Operational Training Unit at RAF Wellesbourne Mountford in Warwickshire. The OTU, along with its satellite airfield a few miles away at Gaydon, was equipped with Wellington aircraft and, as the name implies, it was a training establishment to prepare a 'sprog' for a life fraught with excitement and stress on a squadron. The aircraft allocated to OTUs were mostly from operational squadrons that had made the conversion to the latest four engined types coming on stream, the Halifax and the Lancaster. Many Wimpys had been in service since before the war and were long past their 'best before date'; real nightmares for the engine and airframe fitters whose job it was to keep them flying.

The instructors were veteran aircrew who had completed one, perhaps two, mandatory tours of thirty operations against the enemy and 'screened' on OTU duties for six months: then back to squadrons to chance their luck again for another thirty – against most unfavourable odds. They taught the advanced flying techniques with the emphasis on taking-off and landing – circuits and bumps. The monotony of circuits and bumps was broken by a 'Bullseye' or, occasionally when a maximum effort was planned for a specific enemy target, to make up the numbers in the main force or to carry out a spoof or diversionary raid on a soft target in France. Unfortunately, the Luftwaffe nightfighter pilots and the 88mm anti-aircraft gun crews made no concessions to sprog crews intruding their airspace, consequently there were a proportionate number of OTU casualties. The OTUs provided in excess of 350 aircraft and their crews for the 1,000 bomber raid on Cologne at the end of May 1942, and a number of these aircraft were included in the tally of forty-one that failed to return to their bases from this raid. Most casualties in training were caused in flying accidents where aircraft fell out of the sky because of engine or structural failure, or came to grief through pilot error while performing circuits and bumps. Invariably, the whole crew would perish, including the instructors. These losses tended to weaken the morale of a few of the trainees to the extent that they asked to be taken off flying duties, and they would be quickly posted away overnight. It is a sad fact that the RAF hierarchy treated these poor wretches abominably, classifying them 'Lack of Moral Fibre'; the ignominious label LMF stripping them so unfairly of their self respect. They were stripped of their insignia, and those who did not end up in a psychiatric ward were given the most menial of ground duties. Regardless of the fact that these very stressed airmen were posted in a hurry, those they left behind did not become 'contaminated' by this LMF bug; in fact, the number of men in Bomber Command who found they were unable to cope under pressure with the trials of wartime flying was minimal.

The intake of a course at OTU was made up of equal numbers of the six trades that were necessary to form crews for the medium and heavy aircraft. This was to assist the ritual of 'crewing up'; bringing together complete strangers to train and fly as a team until, fate permitting, the end of the war. The first working day was taken by the pilots choosing a crew from the other aircrew trades assembled in the mess. The recruitment would be by mutual consent and the deal struck with a firm handshake. From experience this method of crewing up proved to be the most satisfactory, and generally ensured that such problems as incompetence, insubordination, serious clashes of personality and, of course, the sudden nervous aversion to air travel, were resolved before a squadron posting. This is the way in which I was introduced to the crew I was to fly with in the months to come, albeit for not so long as I would have preferred.

The pilot, Steve Tomyn, was an amiable Canadian from Alberta, where he had worked on his parents' farm. His grandparents had migrated from the Ukraine just before the turn of the century and settled in the area of a township now known as Two Hills, situated about a hundred miles due east of Edmonton. Steve was stockily built with fair hair and blue eyes. He was inclined to be reserved and quietly spoken, but possessed a strong personality and left his crew in no doubt who was the skipper while we were in the air. At twenty-six years of age, he was the oldest member in the crew. He had, not long before, become engaged to a young lady named Connie who he met while we were at OTU and with whom he had fallen head over heels in love. We were looking forward to their wedding which had been arranged to take place at a registry office ceremony at Leamington Spa on Saturday, 24 April – less than three weeks away.

Geoffrey Hall was the name of the navigator. He was twenty-two years of age, a lanky 6 feet 2 inches in height and a native of Stafford and the Potteries. A softly spoken studious type, he had been a GPO engineer before joining the RAF and volunteering for aircrew. He soon discovered that he was to suffer from air sickness. Despite this handicap, the constant nausea did nothing to prevent us successfully reaching our destination and back within a reasonable estimated time of arrival – ETA, even when experiencing atrocious weather conditions. He should have received a medal for conduct above and beyond the call of duty. Geoff was another one who had the love bug, and whenever possible he would catch a train to be with Joyce, his childhood sweetheart.

Albert Symons was our bomb-aimer. A month or two younger than Steve and at a well-built 5 feet 6 inches he was the shortest member of the crew. A Welshman from South Wales he was, as would be expected, a keen sportsman, particularly as a rugby player. He was conscripted into the Army and sent to the Isle of Wight, but after he had been there a while he decided that army life was not for him and successfully applied for a transfer into the RAF. He was accepted and sailed to South Africa to carry out his training under the Empire Training Scheme. He graduated as an observer which, at that time, was synonymous with the title bomb-aimer. Both he and his fiancée, Dorothy, a resident of the Isle of Wight, were deeply religious and staunch Methodists. On most Sundays he would attend church services, and appeared to prefer his own company to that of other crew members.

The rear-gunner rejoiced in the name of William Ostaficiuk. His forebears left Romania for the plains of southern Alberta, Canada, to farm at Vauxhall near Lethbridge. He was over 6 feet tall, twenty-four years of age, and had a slight build. Being much taller than the average air-gunner, he gave the impression that he was far from comfortable when wedged in the gun turret at the tail end of a Wimpy. If he was uncomfortable, then he was perfectly happy to suffer in silence for the sake of the King and Commonwealth. Although taciturn, he always had a ready smile and a keen sense of humour. We became close friends because, like me, he was single, unattached, and enjoyed a pint of beer and a night on the town. When in town he would seek out a fish and chip shop. Snook fishcakes would send him into raptures.

With a name like Anthony Johnson, but called Tony after the

name of a cowboy's horse featured in the early westerns starring Tom Mix, I was bound to attract the nickname of 'Johnnie' from my crew. Just over twenty years of age, I was a rather skinny 5 feet 11 inches, but still growing. Also of a quiet nature, that is until I had consumed a couple of pints of beer and suffered what can only be described as verbal diarrhoea, I was content to listen rather than do the talking. I was already convinced that one learns more that way.

I spent my youth in London and Essex until I volunteered for the RAF. Leaving school at thirteen years of age I obtained employment at a garage as an apprentice mechanic, or rather grease-monkey, and forecourt attendant, which I kept for four years until my seventeenth birthday. I passed my driving test a month after that birthday and obtained work as a delivery van driver for a butcher at Brentwood. To deliver rationed meat to customers and a few hundredweight of sausages to Warley Mental Hospital soon had me looking for another way to spend my life, and so I joined the RAF.

During just over two years in the RAF I was already beginning to speak posh like the fighter pilots who did so well during the Battle of Britain, and as I was at Brentwood through 1940 I had a front row seat to watch them perform. Jargon like 'Good show, old chap!' and 'Wizard prang . . . what?' was coming naturally, not only to me, but also to Bill who sounded like Noel Coward rehearsing his lines for 'Private Lives'.

I found the time we spent at OTU could be quite nerve-racking especially during the months of November and December 1942, when fog, snow and freezing weather conditions caused all sorts of problems which tested the flying and navigation skills of Steve and Geoff to the full. Icing up in the air was really hazardous, and on too many occasions we would be stooging around blindly searching for a gap in the clouds that could so quickly shroud the airfields of North Yorkshire and Durham. We wanted to make a landing without too much drama, and I would sit in my radio compartment and quietly pray until I felt the landing wheels make contact with terra firma. I would then adopt my 'didn't worry me a bit – piece of cake really' attitude for the benefit of the crew.

Hunched in his turret, Bill was undoubtedly the coldest and loneliest of the crew, his teeth chattering like a runaway teleprinter when he had something to say over the intercom. His inter-flight meal of jam, spam or fish paste sandwiches would freeze so he was unable to bite into them. However, he soon learned to store his food in my compartment until he was ready for a snack. I was the fortunate one, inasmuch as when Barnes Wallis designed the aircraft, he made provision for a hot air duct between the port engine nacelle and the wireless operator's compartment, just under the desk. It was intended to channel the warm air to the forward end of the aircraft, but in practice I was the only one to really benefit. This was the only perk to being a wireless operator/air-gunner, because being covered with fabric, the Wimpy was a cold and draughty aeroplane to travel in over the UK and the Continent.

The twin-engined Vickers Wellington medium bomber first entered service with the RAF in October 1938, and soon became affectionately known as Wimpy after the Popeye cartoon character with a really gluttonous appetite for hamburgers. Following the outbreak of war in 1939 its production was stepped up, along with the two other twin-engined bombers, the Armstrong Whitworth Whitley and the Handley Page Hampden, to equip the growing number of squadrons then carrying out raids against the enemy. Later, as the more successful squadrons began to be equipped with the four-engined heavy bombers, the Short Stirling, the Handley Page Halifax and the Avro Lancaster, the medium bombers began to be slowly phased out of the squadrons operating from bases in the UK – the well tried reliable Wimpy outlasting the Whitley and the Hampden.

While many groups in the south of England went through the process of converting to heavies, the Wimpys and other aircraft they cast off were used to equip the two OTU groups in the Midlands and to make good the operational losses of the squadrons still using medium bombers, particularly 4 and 6 Groups in the north.

It was rumoured that 427 Squadron would soon convert to Halifax aircraft but, until that time arrived, we would have to make do with aircraft obsolescent, and beset by problems brought on by the wear and tear of constant use, resulting in some crews having to abort a sortie long before reaching their targets, or find themselves spiralling out of the sky because of engine failure.

The ten squadrons of 6 Group RCAF were concentrated in the area of countryside forming a corridor between the City of York at its southern end and the Borough of Darlington in the north. About fifteen miles wide, it was flanked by the Great North Road and Pennine Hills to the west and the Cleveland Hills and the North Sea to the east. It was a unique Group because for the most part it was an all Canadian outfit funded by the Canadian tax-payers through their Government in Ottawa. No other Commonwealth air forces serving within the framework of Bomber Command enjoyed such a Group status. Initially it was necessary for approximately thirty-five per cent of the Group's establishment to be drawn from the RAF and other Commonwealth air forces to bring it up to operational strength and efficiency.

The Group was inaugurated on 1 January 1943, and was formed from elements of 4 Group and other Canadian squadrons serving throughout Bomber Command before being brought together in Yorkshire. By March the same year, a total of ten squadrons were operating from eight airfields, with Middleton St George and Leeming each accommodating two squadrons. Of the ten squadrons, three only were operating with the Halifax heavy bombers, and they were very much envied by the Wimpy boys. The Canadians gave each of their squadrons a code name; for instance, Goose, Moose, Tiger, Lion, Ghost and, perhaps appropriately, Alouette for 425 Squadron which had a more than average number of French Canadians in its complement.

The 6 Group Headquarters was based at Allerton Hall, which was not far from the Great North Road at Knaresborough, Yorkshire. It was referred to as 'Castle Dismal' by those senior officers who attended for the daily briefing, because of its stark and forbidding silhouette against the dull wintery skies. Air Chief Marshal G. E. Brookes OBE was the first Air Officer Commanding

17

6 Group, the RAF being very much in command, and was to remain so for the duration of hostilities.

427 (Lion) Squadron was actually formed in October 1942 from a nucleus of six experienced crews from 419 (Moose) Squadron which was operating from Middleton St George. Shortly afterwards, on 7 November, Wing Commander D. H. Burnside DFC took command. By the time it became a part operationally of 6 Group in January 1943 it had the following establishment: 136 RCAF personnel of which seventy were aircrew; 248 RAF personnel of which sixty-two were aircrew; other miscellaneous personnel made the grand total of 419.

Bomber Command's Commander-in-Chief was Air Chief Marshal Sir Arthur Harris. He and his Air Staff were ensconced at the Command's Headquarters at High Wycombe in Buckinghamshire, some 300 miles to the south of Croft. It was at High Wycombe that all the operations were planned and relayed by hot line to the various Group Headquarters and, in turn, passed on to the squadrons at the sharp end. The 'target for tonight' order would reach the squadrons early enough in the day for them to prepare and carry out the raid on the designated target that night. The first eight weeks of 1943 were taken up pounding the submarine pens along the coast of Brittany in France. These important naval bases of Brest, St Nazaire and Lorient were maintaining and supplying the *Kriegsmarine* submarine 'Wolf Packs' that were causing heavy losses to Allied shipping in the Atlantic. Lorient was subjected to nine separate raids during this period, virtually razing the town to the ground.

By mid-March, Arthur or 'Bomber' Harris had turned his attention to the important armament industrial area of the Reich, Essen, Duisburg, Düsseldorf and Cologne. Because this area of Germany was so heavily defended, resulting in the 'chop rate' being uncomfortably high, it paradoxically became known as 'Happy Valley'. The campaign itself was referred to as 'The Battle of the Ruhr' – and it was really some battle. The Ruhr Valley took its toll on Bomber Command.

Our crew joined the squadron in January 1943, but it was still in its embryo stage, understaffed and under-equipped, and feeling its way to becoming an efficient operational unit. Those operations the squadron took part in were carried out by experienced crews, while we sprogs continued to bless our luck and concentrate on training exercises. We would look upon those veterans sporting the DFC and DFM with utmost respect and envy; all well earned medals.

The 'Lion' Squadron soon attracted the interest of the Metro-Goldwyn-Mayer Film Studios who decided to adopt it. We were presented with tunic badges bearing the MGM lion logo, and also passes giving us free admittance to any MGM Cinema. In fact, the film star Clark Gable, himself an air-gunner in the 8th USAAF, would visit Croft and preside over the forthcoming 'adoption' ceremony. There could be no doubt that we were living in exciting times.

Chapter 2

DUISBURG

After breakfast next day, Bill and I rode over to East Vince Moor farm on our RCAF issued bikes to have a look at the crash site and, more importantly, to find out how the Pearson family had fared as a result of a Wellington bomber crashing in front of their farm-house. We had cycled round the perimeter track to the farm on many occasions, usually for elevenses when we could manage it. The farmer's wife, Mary, assisted by her daughter Betty and other members of her family of ten children, was carrying on a lucrative refreshment business from her kitchen. On most mornings there would be a queue of airmen at the back door waiting to purchase egg sandwiches, dripping on toast, cups of tea and glasses of milk at prices the station NAAFI failed to match for quality and value.

As we neared the farm we saw that the wreckage had been removed – to be deposited in a heap beside the maintenance hanger. And at the house we were surprised to discover that it was business as usual, with Mary preparing for the anticipated rush of hungry sightseers and well-wishers. The family appeared none the worse for the previous night's experience, and would soon have the structural damage to the farmhouse fixed. This was most pleasing indeed. Farmer Pearson was never seen about the premises as he was more or less confined to his bedroom with ill health, which, sadly, had not been improved by the untimely death of one of his sons. Albert, a twin, had accidentally been burnt to death whilst cleaning his clothes with petrol in an airman's hut on the airfield.

In view of all the circumstances, Bill and I were amazed at the fortitude of the family, and doubted that anyone could begrudge the extra money it earned with its popular takeaway business venture.

Where the wreckage had been, the surface was covered with a sludge of water saturated debris. Several elm trees had been badly scarred and burnt, in particular the one that had taken the full impact which was in such a dangerous state that it would have to be felled. Looking at the scorched earth, and trying to visualize where Sergeants Ash and Dodds had been sitting at the time of the crash, I was unable to control a surge of emotion that came over me. As we walked to our bikes, I had to wipe away the tears and remind myself that one should not get too personally involved.

The rest of the morning was most likely taken up by a visit to a local swimming baths for a session of dinghy drill or by having to sit through a lecture on how best to evade capture in the event of being shot down over enemy territory.

The prospect of having to ditch an aircraft crippled by enemy action in the sea was very real indeed, and it was essential to learn the art of transferring from a sinking aircraft to a rubber doughnut-shaped dinghy without taking in too much water. At the baths the several crews would change into flying suits and fasten on Mae West inflatable life jackets. Despite the importance of the instruction, many refused to take it seriously. It was not a lot of fun for non-swimmers, and there was at least one with this handicap in each crew.

If members of the public could witness five grown men prancing around the flexible inner-tube shape of a dinghy, and holding hands in the centre like aquatic Old Time Dancers, they would have thought it a strange and comical sight. But the instructors deemed the pantomime necessary for us to gain confidence and to feel at ease in gale lashed freezing seas until, hopefully, rescued by an RAF launch. It was really hilarious to watch some non-swimmers endeavour to bridge ten feet of water between the side of the baths and the dinghy by running and trying to tread water, to be hauled out by the occupants of a dinghy before they fully submerged, because they had neglected to inflate their Mae West. It was all jolly good fun.

The Escape and Evasion lectures usually took place in the afternoon after lunch. A visiting senior officer would impress upon his audience that, in the event of any airmen having the misfortune to bale out the wrong side of the North Sea or English Channel, it was most advisable to hide the parachutes, Mae Wests and aircrew insignia, preferably by burying them, before making tracks in the general direction of Blighty. Equipped with ingenious escape aids, such as a magnetic compass cunningly concealed in a tunic button, or a compass formed simply by balancing one specially adapted battle-dress button upon another, a map of northern Europe printed on a handkerchief square and French, Belgium and Dutch currency, the evader could make every effort to contact a friendly resistance movement. Alternatively, by making for either Switzerland or Sweden one could face the prospect of internment for the rest of the war. Use should be made of the stars at night and road signs for direction finding, and it was much more prudent to travel by night and to go to ground during the hours of daylight. At all costs the evader should avoid contact, or confrontation, with the enemy, especially the dreaded Gestapo or SS.

To give a lecture of this nature so soon after lunch, regardless of the importance of the subject, the speaker would face an audience that showed little or no interest: not one of them would be so unlucky as to be shot down over enemy territory, and consequently heads would loll and eyes would close. I was one of those who, inclined to daydream, would stare into space and completely fail to register the all important points of the lecture – to my eventual cost.

It was during a meal in the canteen one evening that Steve, with obvious embarrassment, made the shock announcement that he and Connie had decided to marry, and the date for the wedding had already been arranged. Whatever our reservations, we were nevertheless delighted at the prospect of attending the wedding – despite the fact that it would put an end to our all-bachelor crew status. We applied to take a week's leave together which, in any event was the most satisfactory arrangement from a practical point of view and following the ceremony the newlyweds would depart for London, and the rest of us would go our separate ways. Steve might even get to use his MGM pass at the Empire, Leicester Square.

Our misgivings about the joining in matrimony of Steve and Connie were based on the fact that the 'chop' rate in our present vocation was frighteningly high with little more than a fifty-fifty chance of survival. During the three and a half months the squadron had been in existence it had lost twelve aircraft on sorties and a total of fifty-two aircrew had been killed. Two of the aircraft had flown into high ground, one into the Cheviot Hills and the other into a peak in Derbyshire. Two crews had wandered off course on their way back from Lorient and got themselves interned in the Republic of Ireland, both aircraft being destroyed. In the same period the Group had lost a total of sixty-four Wellingtons and thirty-one Halifaxes, and 388 aircrew had died in action, 248 of whom were Canadians. At that time we had no idea of the death toll although, at squadron level, we were aware of the aircraft losses. It was not until after the war when all aircrew prisoners of war had been repatriated and debriefed that the full extent of the sacrifice, in terms of human life, made by the crews of Bomber Command became known.

Once a month we had what was rudely called the 'Squadron Piss Up' at the Bull's Head public house in Darlington. Each crew member, except the few teetotallers, chipped in ten shillings and the kitty funded the cost of the party given as a 'thank you' measure for the indispensable ground crews who maintained our aircraft and showed us so much consideration and respect.

Darlington was situated four miles due north of Croft airfield and, quite apart from it being renowned for its main railway and wire manufacturing industries, it boasted that there were more public houses per square mile in the Borough, if not in the whole of the country, then certainly in the north of England. This proved to be an ideal state of affairs to cater for the insatiable thirsts of the airmen from the outlying bomber squadrons at Middleton St George, Croft and Leeming, and the small army of soldiers in training at Catterick Camp a few miles to the south-west.

While it was true that the publicans generally did a good trade with the soldiers and airmen most nights, the aircrew trade depended upon whether or not operations or night flying exercises were being carried out.

The eager party-goers, some with females regardless of the fact that a men only affair was encouraged, would start to arrive at the venue soon after opening time. For these special functions, the landlord let us have the use of a hall on the first floor. This ensured some privacy away from the bars. A wiry white-haired pensioner was retained for the evening to ensure a steady supply of alcohol and sandwiches, for the odd sixpences or few coppers tips from the more well-off Canadian nationals. As the evening wore on the effort in climbing the stairs would become too much for him and, slopping beer all over the place, and quite inebriated, he would get to the first floor landing by the one step up and two or more down method. By this time we were all variously affected by the drink, with everyone shouting above the background noise instead of talking nicely. We were enjoying ourselves.

As the merrymaking got into full swing on one such occasion, a couple of us who were sitting on the edge of the stage, felt the need to examine the contents of a trunk tucked away behind curtains. It was crammed full with the regalia of the Darlington Lodge of the Royal Antediluvian Order of the Buffaloes; horned headdress, ornate chains of office, and the other paraphernalia associated with the Buffs soon adorned the battledress worn by the young lions of 427 Squadron, who went straight into an alcohol inspired Red Indian war dance, a dance so impressive that Geronimo himself would have been cock-a-hoop. With a back-up group of ground-crew braves and parachute section squaws tom-toming away on their chair seats, the dancers whooped and gyrated around the hall. One of the dancers seemed to know what he was doing, because he was out-whooping and out-dancing the rest of us: understandably, because he was a Canadian veteran pilot who could think of no better way of letting his hair down between his forays over enemy territory.

The old man halted in his tracks when he next staggered into

24

the hall with what was left of a full tray of drinks and comprehended what was happening. His jaw sagged with astonishment, while the tray and contents crashed to the floor. This noisy competition brought an abrupt end to this particular bit of off-the-cuff entertainment. By the time the landlord made his appearance, the RAOB property had been stuffed back into the trunk. He was not amused, but rather than turn away lucrative monthly custom he refrained from barring us from the premises on this occasion. A senior officer gave his word that the property in the trunk would not be touched again or retained as souvenirs. As if we would.

When time was called, those who had not arranged other means of transport, made a not too straight and somewhat noisy course along Victoria Road to the railway station. A short train journey ensured that we were in our billets before midnight. Next morning, suffering from hangovers, Bill and I would be reprimanded by the moderate drinkers Steve and Geoff, and the abstainer, Bert.

On Thursday, 8 April, a date I'm not likely to forget, I learned that I was going on my first operation over Germany. This news had my adrenal glands secreting in double time. Steve, Bert and I were to be crewed with a veteran skipper, with Steve as 'second-dicky' sitting on a folding seat and giving his undivided attention, while Bert and I would substitute the usual bomb-aimer and wireless operator. It was normal practice on squadrons to have mixed crews of old hands and sprogs, to baptize the latter before committing them over enemy territory for the first time.

We took our seats in the Briefing Room some fifteen minutes before the briefing was due to begin. The squadron was to provide ten aircraft for the raid and their markings and pilots' names were displayed on the Operations Board for all to see. The fifty plus aircrew taking part were chatting away in groups, but most were unsuccessful in trying to put aside their thoughts on the impending incursion over the Reich. Certainly the few sprog crews present had no doubt that the business of actually venturing into enemy airspace to unload bombs was very risky indeed and the act of pursing one's lips and nonchalantly whistling 'Chattanooga Choo Choo' softly fooled nobody. While some crews were busy playing cards, others were organizing a sweepstake to guess the take-off and landing times of the last aircraft to become airborne – provided it did manage to get back. Some of the experienced crews would be 'shooting the line', mostly for the benefit of the sprog element. We would listen to accounts of such feats as 'the flak was so heavy you could walk on it', 'we flew so low over the target we snagged some fraülein's panties on our tail wheel', 'wave hopping so low over the North Sea that the bomb bay filled with seaweed', and another 'the cloud was so thick over the target that we had to get out and push the kite'. The mind boggled. Listening to the various conversations, such place names as Toronto, Essen, Birmingham, Montreal, St Nazaire and St Albans were the likely ones to be heard.

Despite the sham carefree expression I hoped to convey, I was unable to rid myself of the gnawing anxiety that filled my mind, at least until I took my place in the aircraft and busied myself in carrying out my duties as a wireless operator; an anxiety that compared with the trauma in a dentist's chair before a well embedded molar is extracted, or undergoing a driving test with a demon examiner – sheer terror.

To sprog crews the veterans, who were usually recognized by their shabby battledress and well worn flying boots, appeared highly strung extroverts. Many were the holders of the DFM or DFC, or both. One would go around wearing a stetson, while another wore an eye patch and a stuffed parrot on one shoulder. Although these characters were inclined to be 'way out' they were the revered 'flak happy' warriors who suffered from a condition brought about by over-exposure to the Luftwaffe's attempts to blast them out of the skies over Europe. They were the best at their job, but many were still pushing their luck as they neared the magical score of thirty operations and a break from flak and other targets defences.

Suddenly we were called to attention, an order immediately countermanded by the Commanding Officer of the Squadron, Wing Commander Dudley Burnside DFC, as he entered the room and walked briskly along the aisle followed by his usual retinue of senior officers. The CO drew the curtains covering a large wall map and, indicating the Ruhr, the manufacturing heartland of Germany, announced; 'the target for tonight, gentlemen, is Duisburg'. There was an audible groan from the assembly. The intelligence officer explained that we were going to try and incur even more damage to the iron and steel industry at Duisburg with the primary aim of slowing down, and perhaps grinding to a halt, the Nazi war machine – all stirring stuff. After listening to further briefing from the navigation, wireless, armament and met. section officers we were dismissed with their blessings. Our squadron was to muster ten Wimpys to be included in a main force of over 390 aircraft, both four and twin-engined. We had much to do to occupy ourselves before take-off time around 21.30 hours.

Wing Commander Burnside was thirty-one years of age and, by our standards, was getting a bit long in the tooth, the average age for aircrew being about twenty-two years. He was a regular officer who enlisted in the RAF in the mid-1930s. As a pilot he had logged many hours flying various types of aircraft in the UK and India, the sort of experience so necessary to better the chances of surviving a tour of operations. A fearless and respected CO who, on more occasions than he need, took part in operations invariably selecting the well defended rather than the comparatively easy targets called 'milk runs'; aerial mine-laying called 'Gardening' for instance.

In March, a few months after taking command of the squadron, Wing Commander Burnside and his crew were involved in a particularly 'shaky do', when their aircraft received a direct hit by flak over Essen in the Ruhr. The navigator, Pilot Officer Heather, was standing beside Burnside in the cockpit when the shell exploded immediately beneath them in the, thankfully, empty bomb bay. Pilot Officer Heather took the full blast and died immediately, while the wireless operator, Flight Sergeant Keen had his right foot amputated by a chunk of shrapnel. Another white hot piece of metal almost castrated Burnside as it flew up between his knees to sever his oxygen tube before shattering the windshield at face level, creating hurricane-like conditions in the front of the aircraft. In trying to cope with the sudden and shocking emergency, Burnside failed to notice that his oxygen supply had been cut off until he began to feel light headed. He had little option but to put the stick forward and nose the aircraft into a steep dive to descend to an altitude of around 10,000 feet where it was unnecessary to rely on piped oxygen, and this manoeuvre did nothing to lessen the raging whirlwind in the cockpit. Despite these appalling conditions, the CO managed to nurse the stricken aircraft to an emergency landing field at Stradishall in Suffolk and land, some three hours after Pilot Officer Heather met such a sudden death. In spite of the terrible injury he had received, Flight Sergeant Keen insisted on helping Pilot Officer Hayhurst to plot a course back to the UK.

For his bravery and devotion to duty Geoffrey Keen was awarded the Conspicuous Gallantry Medal and received a commission to Pilot Officer. He would spend many weeks in hospital. Wing Commander Burnside was awarded a Bar to his DFC, and the two other surviving crewmen, Pilot Officers Hayhurst and Ross, the rear gunner, were also awarded the DFC.

When we arrived back to our billet after the briefing, we welcomed some new arrivals to the squadron. They were unpacking their kitbags and were anxious to know all about operations. We decided not to tell them that they were occupying the beds of a crew listed as missing a few nights ago, although Bill and I did 'shoot the line' a bit as we were off to Germany in a couple of hours time.

After writing to my parents, I stowed my personal belongings in my bedside locker. This property included what was left from my last pay parade, except a sole sixpenny piece which I always carried in case we landed at a strange airfield. A sixpence could buy a few cups of NAAFI tea. For the same reason I tucked two packets of cigarettes into my battledress blouse.

After a meal we collected our flying rations for the trip, made up of Spam sandwiches, a bar of chocolate and an orange. There was always an orange which, if stowed in the rear-turret, would freeze as hard as a billiards ball half a mile up in the sky. I would visualize the chief catering officer of the RAF turning up at Covent Garden or Spitalfields fruit and vegetable markets in London at the crack of dawn to select Grade A oranges for the pampered boys of Bomber Command. I suppose, compared to the other two Services and our ground trades, we were inclined to be rather spoilt.

Next I collected the current list of Luftwaffe air to ground radio frequencies and was given some friendly advice from the Signals Officer in connection with the duties I would have to carry out during the trip. I was required to sign for a packet of foreign currency; German Marks, French and Belgian Francs and Dutch Guilders. The exchange rates between these currencies and Sterling were non-existent; this was 'Escape Money' to assist in evading capture and hopefully making a 'Home Run' if shot down over enemy territory.

In the Crew Room we donned our flying gear, the fur-lined Irvin jacket, Mae West and two pairs of gloves, leather gauntlets over white silk. I was already wearing the white woollen submariner-style roll neck sweater under my battle-dress, an item of clothing that was a boon at 20,000 feet. After checking the oxygen masks and earphone cords attached to our flying helmets, we collected our parachutes and Mae Wests from the Parachute Section. We were ready to go to war.

Forty-five minutes before we were due to take off, we were transported out to the aircraft way across the airfield at its dispersal point. We had already been introduced to the crew members we were to accompany to Duisburg that night, pilot, navigator and rear-gunner. I could only envy Geoff and Bill who were being left behind, but, although still feeling a bit queasy, I was ready for my first operation over Germany, to clobber the target with 500 lb bombs and sticks of incendiaries.

Climbing into the aircraft via a short aluminium ladder through the main hatch below the cockpit, I stowed my parachute and went through the procedure of checking the wireless equipment. The interior of a Wellington aircraft can be best described as a sixty feet long tube with egg-shaped bulkheads, the narrowest sections at the top. The airframe was of geodetic construction, or like king-size chicken wire, which was stretch-covered with strong lightweight fabric. Barnes Wallis designed the fuselage so that the crew, apart from the rear-gunner, sat directly above the bomb bay.

29

The pilot sat on an elevated throne in the cockpit, while the wireless compartment was situated below and behind him on the port side. Then with his seat obstructing the gangway, sat the navigator. The bomb-aimer had the option of sitting or standing to the right of the pilot, or getting down to his bomb-aiming position in the nose. Behind the navigator was a camp bed fixed to the floor for whatever use was considered absolutely necessary. Then bridging the fuselage to a height of four feet was the main spar, which, with its two large nuts and bolts not only held the wings together, but also helped to hold the wings to the fuselage. On the port side near the main spar were the master hydraulic cylinders, their pumps being driven by the port engine to operate the undercarriage, flaps, front and rear turrets and bomb doors. Above this was the perspex astrodome with a row of oxygen bottles strapped to the fuselage beside it. Under the oxygen supply was a flare chute which exited by the trailing edge of the starboard wing, and a hand pump to top up the engines with oil during flights of over four hours duration. From the main spar one had to balance along a thirty foot catwalk to the rear of the door giving access to the rear turret. An important design feature on the floor beside the catwalk at the back end of the aircraft was a diamond shaped escape hatch. Because it had a flimsy wooden cover press-studded to the airframe, it was important that it was not accidentally stepped on during take-off, while the aircraft was airborne or landing.

After the engines had reached operating temperature, we left the dispersal pan to join the queue of other aircraft. The pilot did not have long to wait for the green signal, and it seemed in no time at all that we were thundering along the runway; passing the fan club by the Airfield Control Point van, which included the CO, the squadron padre, the Reverend Rockingham, and a bevy of airwomen, some probably seeing their boyfriends or lovers off to war.

Very conscious of the fact that I was sitting over a few thousand pounds of high explosives and lots of incendiary devices, I was relieved to feel the aircraft take to the air during those vital seconds after reaching flying speed. All our squadron aircraft participating in the raid were airborne about 21.30 hours, with about thirty seconds between each take-off. Circling to climb over the high ground of the Yorkshire Moors, we set course on the first leg to a position over the North Sea off Flamborough Head to rendezvous with other squadron aircraft streaming towards the Continent. Apart from the navigator and myself, who would be otherwise engaged, the crew would be keeping a sharp lookout for other aircraft. The skies over eastern England from Durham in the north to Suffolk and Norfolk further south, would be swarming with aircraft climbing to reach their predetermined height, and heading on course to converge over the North Sea to form a stream of over 390 units hell bent on destruction; a stream that cruised between 130–140 mph, forming a corridor up to 100 miles long by twenty miles wide, at heights varying from 5,000 to over 20,000 feet. This bomber force was preceded by the elite Pathfinder Force from 8 Group to identify and mark the targets with coloured indicator flares.

The air activity over eastern England had not gone unnoticed by the enemy. The Luftwaffe manning Freya radar scanners would soon be able to predict the flight path of the incoming bomber force. Messerschmitt Bf 110 and Junkers Ju88 twin-engined night-fighters, equipped with Lichtenstein radar which was effective for up to four miles, would be scrambled from their airfields in Holland and Belgium to await and intercept the 'Tommy' aircraft. Coupled with the Freya radar was the short-range Würzburg radar which, although only efficient for a radius of twenty miles, was a most useful piece of equipment because it gave the altitude in addition to the direction of an aircraft.

The nightfighters would climb to the height where the bulk of the enemy would be anticipated, and then orbit a radio beacon which, in effect, confined them to their allotted airspace which coincided with the twenty miles radius of the Würzburg scanner. By bringing together two blips on the radar screen, the ground controllers would talk the pilots to the enemy aircraft; the night-fighter navigator most likely picking up a blip on his Lichtenstein set during the last two or three miles from the target and 'fine tuning' his pilot to it. Once sighted, the RAF invariably lost another bomber and its crew as the nightfighter pilot opened up

31

with his 20mm cannons. There would be an almost unending chain of these defensive units stretching along the coast from north Germany through Holland and Belgium, to France. A similar means of air defence, coupled with radar controlled anti-aircraft guns, protected the important cities of the Reich within the range of Bomber Command.

Soon after we crossed the Dutch coast, I began picking up the gutteral sounding voices of the Luftwaffe ground to air radio controllers. Their voices were intermittent and interrupted by deafening interference. The wireless operators in the bombers flying ahead were already 'Tinselling'; the only countermeasure they had to lessen the chances of a nightfighter being directed on to us. I decided that it was time to put my months of training to the test and get in on the act. Setting my transmitter to one of the 'active' Luftwaffe frequencies, then by the simple process of switching a microphone housed in the port engine nacelle to the selected channel and pressing the morse key, the full blast of an enclosed 1,000 Bristol Pegasus engine would swamp any ground to air conversations. If accurately transmitted, the 'Tinsel' caused havoc, and relations between the nightfighter crews and their ground controls would become strained – they would become extremely miffed with us, too. Although many aircraft would be lost during the raid, we received satisfaction that many more would escape a fiery ending by the spoiling nature of the 'key bashers' of Bomber Command. While it could be quite amusing to listen to the Germans losing their cool by being constantly jammed, it also kept a wireless operator's mind off what was happening outside the aircraft.

After passing through the nightfighter defence 'boxes' we flew over the many flak sites, the anti-aircraft gun defences strung out along the route overflown to the target and, as we approached the Ruhr, these sites became more and more plentiful. The Luftwaffe's main ground-to-air defensive weapon was the radar controlled 88mm anti-aircraft gun, or *Flugabwehrkanone*. With an experienced crew it was capable of firing twenty 18lb shells a minute to a height of five miles in twenty-five seconds. Also radar controlled and working in unison with the flak sites were the master searchlights; easily recognized by their blue tinged beams. The master searchlight would lock on to a hapless 'Tommy' aircraft, and then the white beamed searchlights would swing in to cone the aircraft until it was hit by flak or fighter aircraft or the pilot managed to escape into the shadows by performing such aerobatics that no aircraft designer possibly envisaged.

It was not until we were approaching Duisburg that I managed to leave my wireless sets and to witness for myself what was going on outside the aircraft. There seemed to be an awful lot of cloud about; weather unfavourable for accurate bombing. There were a number of searchlights to be seen in every direction through 360 degrees about the aircraft which was flying at 18,000 feet; there were also sporadic bursts of flak except for straight ahead where all hell was breaking loose over the target area. In what seemed no time at all I was staring down into Duisburg, a frightening sight to behold for a sprog. Through broken cloud over the whole area there was a pall of smoke and an awesome scintillating display by the pyrotechnics of death and destruction, not only on the ground where it was widespread, but also in the air where search-lights, either probing or in cones, formed a backdrop for innumerable shell bursts, exploding flares and a lone fiery comet arching earthwards. It was awesome and I found myself wanting to avert my eyes away from this activity which was so alien to me. As Bert gave instructions to the pilot lining up for the bomb run, I was only too pleased to take up a position by the flare chute. It was necessary to ensure that the photo-flare did not get hung up in the chute, when it should be following the bombs earthwards. With a short delay fuse activated as it moved down the chute, it was imperative that if it did get hung up a frantic effort should be made to get it on its way. I was given to understand that a hefty shove usually did the trick, otherwise so many million candle power would make the fabric covered Wimpy light up like a monstrous glowworm, causing all sorts of problems for the crew. The flare left the chute without a hitch, and I hoped that we had managed to get a nice snap of the target area through a gap in the clouds. This would please the photographic section and the squadron intelligence officer, as it would prove we had in fact reached and bombed the target.

Our aircraft, having shed its bomb load, seemed anxious to get home. I became engrossed in 'tinselling' as we passed through the nightfighter zone, and it seemed that in no time at all we were crossing the North Sea again, although in fact nearly three hours had elapsed since we crossed the Dutch coast on our outward flight to the target.

We eventually landed at Croft during the early hours of the morning and, after watering the daisies, attending a de-briefing session, having a meal of bacon and fried lumpy eggs, we were off to bed.

Whilst we had completed the trip unscathed, two other 427 Squadron aircraft had to abort the raid early because they experienced icing up conditions. The summary of all the records kept by the squadrons taking part in the raid would show that a total of twenty-one aircraft were missing with a death toll of 138 aircrew. There were fourteen survivors: thirteen became prisoners of war, and one, Pilot Officer Marion RCAF, successfully evaded capture and managed a 'home run' back to Blighty.

Chapter 3

MAXIMUM EFFORT – MANNHEIM

There were many things I would rather do than to go to a funeral but, with little persuasion from the Signals Officer, I agreed to act as a pallbearer at Sergeant James Dodds' funeral, to be carried out with full military honours, at Stranton Cemetery, West Hartlepool. In the meantime, Steve and Bill would attend the funeral of a fellow Canadian, Sergeant Ash, at Carmel Road Cemetery in Darlington.

The service and the interment were highly emotional affairs, and my heart went out to James Dodds' family and friends; there was a large gathering for the local lad. This was not so for Sergeant Ash's funeral twenty miles away where, due to the exigencies of war, none of his family were able to make the journey from Canada to pay their last respects.

Both these municipal cemeteries have large plots of ground set aside for the graves of the military personnel killed on active service. The many Commonwealth airmen from the airfields in the vicinity brought back from raids dead or fatally injured, are laid to rest in these cemeteries alongside the British airmen, soldiers and seamen. It was some comfort to see that these plots were well maintained and each grave had a suitable epitaph on the white standard military headstone.

On the way back to Croft, I dropped off at Darlington and, for something better to do, I went to the cinema hoping to cheer myself up a bit.

After watching the film, I walked the short distance to the Hole in the Wall public house in Market Street. I hitched onto my usual stool at one end of the bar and ordered a beer. The woman at the piano was already pounding out her favourite singalong songs although, with so few customers in the bar at that time, she might just as well have been doing her ironing. For the next hour or so I sat drinking and smoking myself out of the bout of depression, and watching the bar fill to capacity. The dense haze of tobacco smoke made it difficult to see to the far end of an already dimly lit bar.

Draining my glass, I decided to get some fresh air and then set forth on a pub crawl which, in Darlington, simply meant moving from one pub to another around the Market Square. One could diversify by exploring the side street taverns. As I was about to visit the toilet before leaving, I noticed a party of three Women's Land Army girls elbowing their way to the bar. I immediately took a fancy to the one ordering drinks. She was beautiful, with blue eyes set in a radiant oval face with a peaches and cream complexion; shoulder length blonde wavy hair hung from beneath a jauntily worn pork pie shaped Land Army hat. We were attracted to one another the moment our eyes met, and I completely dismissed the notion to breathe fresh air and embark on a pub crawl. Eat you hearts out Betty Grable, Alice Faye, and all the many other glamorous film stars I had until then secretly adored. I was suddenly infatuated with someone else with a Geordie accent.

Due to exigencies of flying duties during the seven days following the funerals of Sergeants Ash and Dodds, I managed to get into Darlington to see Joyce on a couple of occasions only. Nevertheless our romance blossomed.

We were placed on standby for a maximum effort to target Frankfurt during the night of the 8–9 April, but in the event the squadron could only dispatch ten aircraft out of the anticipated sixteen which had been fitted with long-range petrol tanks necessary for them to complete a round trip to the target. Our aircraft was one of those still waiting for these tanks which had been ordered some weeks ago in early March before the Squadron was equipped with Wellington Mk Xs to replace the faithful, albeit battle fatigued, Mark IIIs.

We were put on standby for a raid on Stuttgart a couple of nights later, but once again our participation was not required; this time because only ten aircraft from the squadron were required to be deployed. However, before take-off that night there were two cases of careless driving. In the first, a taxiing aircraft crashed into a petrol bowser and on the second, quite by sheer coincidence, a bowser was driven into an aircraft at its dispersal. Both aircraft and bowsers were temporarily unserviceable, and the Commanding Officer was furious. Whilst none of our squadron were posted as missing on the Frankfurt and Stuttgart raids, 6 Group lost four and eight aircraft respectively, resulting in a total of thirty-one airmen killed in action, twenty-seven becoming prisoners of war, and two evading capture.

In the mess one evening we heard a rumour that London Southwood, a sergeant pilot, whose aircraft had not returned from the St Nazaire raid six weeks before, was interned in the Republic of Ireland with his crew and, apparently, was having the life of Riley. This was the first we knew of, not only Southwood's, but also another of our squadron crews, being interned, although not through official channels. A girlfriend of one of the two crews had received correspondence from Eire and was overjoyed to know of his, and nine other crew members' safety. The chiefs would have known this soon after the event, but like so many cover-ups during wartime, kept it from the braves for fear of more crews finding their way to a neutral country, particularly one with a good supply of Guinness. It was assumed that the two aircraft could have suffered damage by enemy action, or a combination of navigational errors, fuel shortage or radio trouble in losing their way back from France and, by an unusually strange coincidence, found themselves over Dublin Bay before flying west inland and abandoning their aircraft as fuel ran out. Both aircraft were write-offs. Sergeant Southwood had previously written off a Wellington aircraft, the first to be lost to the newly formed squadron, during the previous November. While coming in to land at Croft, he had overshot the runway and pancaked the aircraft into a ploughed field. In both cases he and his crew had escaped with minor injuries. It came to pass that these two 427 Squadron crews were the only Bomber Command airmen to find sanctuary from the trials and tribulations of war by being interned in the Republic of Ireland throughout the Second World War, although several crews enjoyed the hospitality of Sweden after running into trouble bombing the North Sea and Baltic Ports.

During this period we occupied some of our time by carrying out dinghy drill at Darlington Swimming Baths (most essential with the North Sea and English Channel between us and our targets in Europe), air tests and other training exercises. One day aircrew had to parade to be issued brand new Raleigh cycles and I am sure some of the Canadians, particularly the French Canadians, had never used a cycle before in their lives. It was quite comical to see the antics of some who tried to maintain their balance with the pedals still turned inwards as they had left the factory. Nevertheless, the cycles provided the means of transport between airfield sites and, in particular, the farm for tea and egg sandwiches. It became immediately necessary to paint some sort of identification on the rear mudguard; in my case 'Lucky Johnnie', to prevent short or long term borrowing without the consent of the keeper.

One morning we climbed into our aircraft to carry out a night flying test, a test that usually took about an hour. Any faults discovered would be reported to the appropriate groundcrew tradesmen to be rectified. Climbing over the main spar towards the rear of the fuselage, I was puzzled to see that a large nut had become loosened on its bolt, one of two bolts virtually holding the wings to the fuselage. The bolt was the upper one and any further vibration would have caused it to unscrew from the remaining exposed few threads. Located at the very centre of the main spar, the castellated nuts were tightened to a specific torque and secured with split pins. In the unlikely event that the aircraft needed a wing replacement, then there would be a practical reason for working on these bolts. The matter was reported immediately to the ground crew and the air test, was, obviously, cancelled. Not one of our ground crew could give a logical answer as to what had happened.

In this instance the gremlins had been really naughty on picking on our aircraft. I would often visualize us taking off, and the flexing motion of the wings dislodging the nut and bolt with quite spectacular consequences: wings slowly folding Pegasus shape, and having lost its aerodynamic properties, the misshapen Wimpy would plunge earthwards, the hapless crew unable to escape because they would be subjected to powerful 'G' forces.

We were all perfectly aware that, despite the guard patrols, the airfield security was almost non-existent, except when trying to sneak past the guardroom by the main gate. The perimeter fence could be breached in many places, and used to provide a short cut across the airfield from Croft Spa Hotel or the railway station. We were more inclined to put the incident down to sabotage by an enemy sympathizer who could also enter the airfield many ways rather than having to pass the guardroom. The children at West Vince Moor farm clambered about inside the aircraft parked near their farmhouse most Sundays, as inquisitive youngsters would, but not to use a torque wrench on nuts and bolts. The incident remained a mystery, but I would carry out a most thorough check the next few times we had to fly. I fully supported the belief expressed within the Group that there were hoteliers and boarding house keepers in York, Harrogate and Darlington who, innocently or otherwise, harboured enemy agents registering in such names as Smith, Jones, Thomas, McDonald and O'Reilly; how else could the Luftwaffe obtain the early information of targets selected for attention by Bomber Command; information that would allow them to relocate their nightfighter squadrons and the mobile 88mm anti-aircraft guns. If the saboteurs were RAF personnel, then they were not likely to be aircrew for obvious reasons. Whether the infiltration of enemy agents believed to be infesting our off-duty drinking haunts was an exaggeration or not, one would have to be rather naive to dismiss out of hand the possibility that there were those characters in our midst who were actively engaged in espionage and sabotage. In many cases we could be wrong in planting the blame for unexplained faults and fatal mishaps squarely on the shoulders of gremlins.

On Friday, 16 April, we learned that we were on ops that night.

I started to whistle 'Chattanooga Choo Choo', and then busied myself writing to Joyce in endearing terms and to let her know that I anticipated being with her the following night. A 2½d stamp ensured that she would get it first thing Saturday morning. I wrote other letters, but left them with my personal belongings with what cash I had in my pockets – except a sixpenny piece. I then bulged out by battledress with three packets of 20 Sweet Caporal cigarettes. I was nearly ready to go to war again.

At briefing we were honoured by the presence of Air Vice-Marshal G. E. Brookes, the Officer Commanding 6 Group RCAF, who had popped over from 'Castle Dismal' to make a routine inspection of the squadron. Not only was there an extra large assembly of aircrew, but there was also an exceptional turnout of officers. It was probably a coincidence that Air Vice-Marshal Brookes decided to sit in on the briefing too.

The target for the night was Mannheim situated on the east bank of the Rhine, but just across the river on the west bank was the twin town of Ludwigshafen. Mannheim was a river port and industrial town at the junction of the Rhine and Neckar rivers: it had large electrical, chemical, engineering and textile industries, all of which were essential to the German war machine. 6 Group were committing a total of ninety-one aircraft to the force of 271 Wellington, Stirling and Halifax aircraft. Our squadron's contribution was fourteen aircraft, a maximum effort which accounted for the extra crews at the briefing. Our target was the IG Farben plant at Ludwigshafen.

Another force of 327 Lancaster and Halifax aircraft were going to be with us along the way, but would press on to attack the Skoda works at Pilsen in Czechoslovakia. This plant was manufacturing tanks for the Panzer divisions of the Wehrmacht.

Take-off time for the lead aircraft from Croft was 21.00 hours, with an ETA on target at 01.00 hours. The 8 Group Pathfinder Force of Mosquito and Lancaster aircraft would precede the main force to identify and mark the targets with TI flares. Our squadron would be bombing at heights varying between 18,000 and 21,000 feet, and the met. officer forecast 8/10ths cloud over our route, with a possibility that it would clear to 4/10ths over the target area. If this was to be believed we would have near ideal conditions to reach the target, with the cloud suddenly breaking to give good bombing visibility. As so often happens, the weather over the Continent is nothing like that forecast and aircrews tend to be very sceptical when being shot up by enemy nightfighters in bright moonlight when they were given a forecast of cloud. The met. men had no control over the weather, and their forecasts left a lot to be desired even over the British Isles much less the Continent, where they received no cooperation from their opposite numbers in Germany and occupied Europe.

Our crew was to bomb on green TI flares from virtually our ceiling height of 21,000 feet and, being nearly four miles above the target it would be more luck than judgement, with all due respect to Bert's bombing prowess, to score direct hits. With nearly 300 aircraft off-loading bombs and incendiaries on Mannheim and Ludwigshafen hoping to saturate the docks and industrial areas, it would inevitably develop into the now accepted 'area bombing' in which the civilian population suffered – just as the civilian populations suffered during the blitzkriegs of Warsaw, Amsterdam, Coventry and London. The height we were allocated was virtually the ceiling for a fully bomb laden Wimpy and, with a round trip of some 1,000 miles, we were going to have to watch the fuel gauges. With a full load of 500lb high explosive bombs and racks of incendiaries – weighing something like four tons, there was no room left to accommodate an auxiliary fuel tank.

Once away from the Briefing Room we expressed misgivings about the night's programme. We mere servants of Bomber Command were convinced that the hierarchy at High Wycombe were dispatching us on a diversionary raid to take the 'flak' off the main force of four-engined aircraft sent to wipe out the Skoda Works at Pilsen. By taking the unusual step of selecting two main targets to be attacked the same night, with almost identical flight-paths to both targets, although Pilsen was a further 200 miles beyond Mannheim, we suspected that we were being set up as decoys to attract the malice of the Luftwaffe nightfighter pilots while the main stream pressed on to Pilsen. In any event, with a total of 589 aircraft heading in the general direction of Mannheim

41

and Pilsen, there was bound to be fun and games with the Luftwaffe defences within the next few hours.

For security's sake, after briefing we were confined to camp. We went to collect and sign for escape money, but were told that because the whereabouts of some signatories was unknown, and the squadron had marshalled so many aircraft in a maximum effort, all foreign currency had been issued already.

Soon after 20.00 hours we were conveyed out to our aircraft to carry out the pre-flight check before joining the queue at the end of the runway for the signal to take-off. On checking the wireless equipment I found that the gremlins had been at work again. This time they had rendered both the TR9 air to ground radio transmitter and the IFF, Identification Friend or Foe, equipment unserviceable. The latter piece of equipment was essential as it transmitted a code to deter our own flak batteries from mistaking us for the enemy. We treated our ack-ack gunners with the same respect as their German counterparts, as they could be equally as accurate when they put their minds to it.

We were driven poste-haste to one of the standby aircraft dispersed half a mile around the perimeter. Its fuselage letters were ZL-G. As we climbed into the aircraft I was far from satisfied with the way things were going, although at least the wireless equipment was serviceable and the main spar nuts and bolts were intact. I silently cursed the gremlins whose antics had caused us to switch to an aircraft we knew nothing about. And if I could have foreseen that it would be two years before I would set foot on Blighty soil again I would certainly have declined to fly that night; I would have been struck down with an acute attack of colic and reported sick, or perhaps completely funked out and been branded LMF. Despite giving the aircraft only a cursory inspection, Steve signed the Form 700 which, in effect, charged him with responsibility for the aircraft as viewed and tested. The form was handed back to the ground crew NCO who wished us bon voyage and that the goods would be returned intact. Having satisfied himself that the makeshift aircraft was capable of sustained flight, Steve started the engines to give them time to warm up. Geoff sorted out and spread his charts on the table, and checked the 'GEE'; while

Bill settled in his gun turret. Bert had little to do but assist Steve if necessary. Soon other aircraft were on the move vacating their dispersal sites and taxiing past us to join the queue for take-off. We took our place behind them.

Precisely at 21.15 hours Steve lifted the Wimpy off the runway and began a climbing circuit of the airfield. Once again I was secretly relieved when the aircraft came unstuck from the ground and, complete with heavy bomb load, began a steady climb to follow most of our squadron's aircraft who had been ahead in the queue. Records would show that all 427 Squadron's aircraft became airborne in sixteen and a half minutes flat, breaking all previous records of take-off times.

Wing Commander Burnside and Air Vice Marshal Brookes joined the party at the chequered hut to wave us off, and the AVM must have been suitably impressed by our eagerness to leave Croft and to disrupt the enemy's production schedule.

Soon we were approaching the enemy coast, flying in clear weather as we climbed to 21,000 feet. Geoff would give Steve a course of 130 degrees at Flamborough Head to cross the coast of Holland just south of Rotterdam.

Over the North Sea Steve gave his consent for Bill to fire off a few rounds to test his guns, and a short burst from his four 8mm Browning machine guns resounded through the fuselage; an exercise I considered was enough to alert the Luftwaffe defences throughout Holland and Belgium – but essential to boost his confidence with the assurance that he possessed devastating firepower at his fingertips.

I 'tinselled' like mad while we passed through the Kammhuber Line of the defensive air 'boxes', each with its predatory night-fighter. The Germans referred to the individual 'box' as a *Himmelbett*, our four-poster bed, and the whole system was the brainchild of the Luftwaffe General of nightfighters, Joseph Kammhuber. As soon as I was sure that we had cleared the area of greatest danger before the target, I pumped oil to top up the supply to both engines, after which I took up position in the astrodome.

So far the flight had been uneventful. Visibility was good,

although I was concerned to see that we were leaving telltale vapour trails at the height we were cruising. I reported heavy flak and many searchlights away over to our starboard side, which Geoff suggested would most likely be the town of Saarbrücken. We assumed that either one of our stream had wandered off course or the Pilsen bound bomber stream were overflying the area. With a moonlit night and cloud patches beneath us, flying at our height had its advantages and disadvantages. Nightfighters, like most aircraft, increased fuel consumption dramatically in climbing to reach the upper altitudes, consequently the pilots tended to seek out their prey at much lower levels to give them more flying time before having to land to refuel. From 5,000 up to 15,000 feet, there were comparatively easy pickings to be had among the bulk of the bomber stream flying at these levels. Other advantages were that there was considerably less chance of 'friendly fire', of being bombed by an aircraft or of a mid-air collision. Flak and searchlights could be a problem no matter at what height an aircraft of Bomber Command flew.

Turning slowly full circle I scanned the moonlit sky straining my eyes to spot the glow from an exhaust manifold, or reflected moonlight from a cockpit canopy or a gun turret. If I had spotted anything suspiciously like a nightfighter, there would have been a lot of mental stress as Steve took evasive action by corkscrewing the aircraft, an experience not unlike a ride on the Big Dipper at Blackpool.

As we approached Ludwigshafen, I was mesmerized by the growing intensity of the flak and the increasing number of searchlights that ringed the target area. No matter which way I looked, there was flak exploding all over the sky and black puffs of smoke from shell bursts hung all around the aircraft. I softly whistled 'Chattanooga Choo Choo' into my oxygen mask, and wanted to get away from it all as soon as possible.

Ludwigshafen and Mannheim across the Rhine were really getting clobbered by many tons of high explosives and incendiaries; there were fires that spread over the towns and surrounding areas, and a thick pall of black smoke hung in the air making target marking difficult. TI flares hung above our target area, and clusters of bombs exploded on unseen places far below. With a myriad of shell bursts around us, coupled with the tracer-like effect of light flak, it was an awesome sight, and we were going to have to spend the next few minutes right in the thick of it. I counted two aircraft that would not be returning to their bases, both were on fire and falling out of the sky. There was also a huge explosion about half a mile away on our port side. This could only have been a fully bombed up aircraft receiving a direct hit, and most likely the crew would have been instantly blown to oblivion.

Soon I was aware that the bomb doors were opening and Bert went in to his left . . . left . . . right . . . left routine as he lined the aircraft up for the run to the target. The smoke over the area was causing difficulties, and he asked Steve to go round again. To circle the target, even at the height we were flying, could be compared to driving along a motorway in the wrong lane without lights in pitch darkness. Steve took the aircraft in an orbit and, once again we flew over the huge barbecue. This time we got it right.

With the green TIs drifting along his bombsight, Bert thumbed the bomb release button and announced that the bombs had gone as our kite, now free of its load, reared and performed like a race-horse leaving the starting gate. I watched the photoflash cannister disappear down the chute, while Bill needlessly informed anyone listening that there was a helluva lot of shit coming up and we should get to goddam hell out of the lousy place fast. Steve obliged by making a banking turn from the target area, and Geoff gave him a course to steer on the first leg home. All we had to do now was to successfully run the gauntlet of enemy air defences for another three hours and there would be a bacon and egg break-fast waiting for us at Croft.

We were just leaving the target area when suddenly the aircraft was caught in the beam of a master searchlight, the cockpit being bathed in its eerie light blue fluorescent glow. We were fully in the spotlight for the flak crews to see – we were so vulnerable. We were in deep trouble, and before the other searchlights swung to lock on to us, Steve gave us another roller-coaster ride described by some as chucking the kite about the sky until the searchlight was shaken off. Steve was lucky inasmuch as he managed to shake the searchlight off in less than a minute of violent evasive action, during which time I was glad of the main spar for support. As suddenly as we were caught by the searchlight, we were free from it and back in the comparative safety of the hazy moonlight. Steve could be heard panting with exertion over the intercom; for to have escaped from the menace of the searchlight so soon called not only for muscle power but for a lot of flying skill – and luck. We were all feeling immensely relieved after this latest bit of excitement; Geoff tugged at my trousers and with a wide grin gave the thumbs up sign. We had successfully overcome our first real challenge, and perhaps thwarted the undivided attention of the 88mm radar-controlled flak batteries, or a nightfighter pilot. With all the aerobatics I was rather surprised that Geoff had not thrown up over the aisle behind his seat.

Leaving the main action behind us, we still had to fly through a flak barrage that, although lacking in intensity, was too close for comfort. Looking down from the astrodome, the dark patches of smoke left by the exploding shells formed a panoramic polka-dot pattern against a backcloth of moonlit cloud. I realized that I had lost my fear of flak, just so long as it kept far away from our kite. One 88mm shell came too near.

I was about to return to my wireless compartment to resume 'tinselling' when simultaneously with a loud explosion beneath the starboard wing, it seemed that a giant fist had delivered an uppercut; the aircraft actually flipped onto its back and then screamed nose down in a terrifying spiral dive. I was thrown across the fuselage to land heavily against the hydraulic cylinders, my oxygen mask and intercom microphone being torn from my helmet in the process. An unseen force pinned me to the cylinders in the squat position; meanwhile Geoff and one or two of his navigation instruments momentarily levitated above his seat, before he too was subjected to overwhelming 'G' forces. The howl of the engines was ear-piercing, in truth, as our Wimpy screamed earthwards. A heavy vibration set in and I added the fact that the aircraft may be disintegrating to my troubles; I was quite unable to move to reach my parachute even if it was possible to bale out. Even though I was in a state of shock, I was still aware that at any moment I would be compacted along with the aircraft as it made a crater in German soil. Surely this could not be happening to me when I had just met the girl of my dreams. I unashamedly turned to God for salvation, and he listened to my prayer.

I suddenly became aware of a reduction in noise and vibration, and was relieved to find that I could move about again. Steve was excelling himself this trip as, with super-human effort he had managed to gain control and restore the aircraft to level flight. We had spiralled out of control for a total of 11,000 feet, or two miles, and the fact that the aircraft had not fallen apart, although the starboard engine had been knocked out, was testimony to its rugged design.

I got to my feet and connected up my intercom. Happiness was still being alive. Geoff had vomited.

Chapter 4

Earning a Caterpillar

I hastily scanned the upper surfaces of the plane but was unable to spot any apparent damage, except that the two engines were unserviceable. The airscrew of the starboard engine was stationary, it having either been knocked out by whatever had hit the aircraft or it had raced itself to destruction in the dive. The port airscrew was still spinning, but the engine sounded like a maladjusted lawnmower and was undoubtedly on its way out. The aircraft was close to stalling, and it was necessary for Steve to keep its nose down to maintain flying speed – a situation that could not possibly last much longer.

Bert and I made a hurried check of the petrol and oil cocks and found them to be OK. There would be no advantage in jettisoning movable equipment as flying time could now be measured in minutes. Being unable to revive the engines, Steve gave the order to abandon aircraft.

Nothing was going right. I got a bit excited again when I made a dive for my parachute pack and discovered that it was missing from the bunk where I had left it. Collecting my torch from the wireless compartment, I was relieved to find the pack lying on the catwalk near the rear turret. I told Steve that I would use the rear escape hatch. Discarding my helmet and clipping on my parachute, I wrenched away the safety guard of the escape hatch and stamped out the exit panel – sending it flying into space. By this time Bill had emerged from his turret and we stood face to face over the hole in the floor of the fuselage. There was no time to toss a coin to decide who should jump first so, with quick thinking, I thrust my torch in his hands and unceremoniously dropped out of the aircraft. I was later to discover that I was the first crew member out.

I started to tumble as soon as I hit the slipstream, and I pulled the ripcord as soon as I had judged that I was clear of the tailplane. The canopy blossomed into a lifesaving mushroom which instantly checked my rapid descent. Gyrating considerably slower earthwards, I was amazed by the uncanny silence compared to the bedlam I had experienced during the previous ten minutes. It was so quiet I could hear the gentle rustle of the parachute shroud lines as the chute drifted on the breeze. From high above I could hear the steady drone of the bomber stream making for home – and so much closer to the ground the clatter of a noisy lawnmower fading into the distance.

In the sky where I would have expected Bill to be, I caught a momentary glimpse of another parachute canopy in the moon-light. In the excitement of the occasion I nearly made the mistake of shouting to him, but it would have been most inadvisable to advertise our presence by trying to make ourselves heard over a distance of up to a quarter of a mile. In the middle distance I could make out the River Moselle meandering through a valley, the moonlight on its surface giving it a silvery snake-like effect.

It could not have been more than ninety seconds after I had pulled the ripcord before I made an unscheduled and ungraceful touchdown between rows of grapevines. The risers of my harness had pinned the collar of my Irvin jacket round my head making downward visibility difficult, resulting in a blind approach with a heavy landing. However, I was unhurt apart from minor bruising.

For several minutes I sat straining my ears to pick up any sign of activity suggesting that the hunt for me was on. All I could hear was the faraway sound of a retreating bomber force. My feelings swiftly changed from elation at still being alive to abject loneliness at being so isolated from my loved ones. I sat trying to collect my thoughts but only added anxiety to my feelings. I was anxious that the rest of my crew had managed to survive; that my parents would not believe the worst when they received the telegram to inform

49

them that I was missing in action; and, perhaps selfishly, that Joyce would understand when I failed to keep the date that evening and that she would wait to hear from me. Even despite the fact that we had known one another for only a week, I dismissed the thought that wartime romances sometimes proved quite fragile where long absences were involved.

Using my Irvin jacket as a shield, I lit up a Sweet Caporal and took a few long drags on it. I needed that fag. I decided to make for Luxembourg which I reckoned to be within reasonable walking distance, and there hopefully try to contact some burgher sympathetic to the Allies' cause. Via a well organized escape route I could be back in Blighty before I was much older. How I wished I had been further up front in the queue for escape money back at Croft.

After ripping off my sergeant's chevrons and aircrew insignia from my battledress, I concealed them with my parachute under some vines. The escape and evasion lecturer at Croft would have preferred that I buried the lot, but as the ground was rock hard and I had neglected to bring a pick and spade, it really was too nail tearing and time consuming to abide by his teachings.

I set forth westwards hoping that I might meet up with Steve, Bill or another member of the crew. I had not walked for many minutes before I found myself in a cobblestoned yard with buildings on three sides and a high wall on the remaining side of the quadrangle. I found a gate in the wall which gave access to a narrow lane, and a dog suddenly barking nearby hastened my exit from the yard into the lane.

I was so intent on trying to get out of the place before the dog aroused its masters, that I failed to notice a small group of people standing a few yards down the lane. Tiptoeing away from the door, I was practically on top of them before I realized I was in trouble. We stood staring speechlessly at one another until, to show them that I was an agreeable sort of person, I handed round a packet of cigarettes. Not only did they decline my offer, but they began to make hostile noises and backed off towards one of the cottages behind them.

They were advancing in years and I guessed that they had been in the lane watching the air raid or organizing search parties. As one of the menfolk made a dash for a cottage, I decided not to hang around any longer. I turned on my heels and ran hell for leather down the lane, realizing that the balloon had gone up and a hunt for me would soon be in progress.

Once I was well away from the village I took to the vineyards and meadows, alternately jogging and walking until I collapsed with exhaustion. As I stretched out on the ground, I heard the mournful sound of the all-clear in the distance. The sound of the sirens was no different from those at home. Away to the east there was a lurid red glow in the sky from the devastated Mannheim and Ludwigshafen.

After I had regained my breath, I set off again over a sweet smelling and pleasant undulating countryside. Here and there were clumps of trees as the vineyards disappeared. Unlike the English countryside there were very few hedgerows. The going was good, more so when I came upon a railway track that also led in the direction I wanted to go. Making good use of the expertise I had acquired on the LNER between Eryholme Junction and Croft, I bounded along the sleepers at a canny speed. On two occasions I had to dive in the undergrowth beside the track while freight trains squeaked and clattered past, but this proved to be a blessing as I needed the rest. I had to be particularly careful at level crossings, and felt it wise to bypass railway stations. At one time I was bounding along parallel with a road, when a convoy of military vehicles passed; perhaps a weary search party returning to its barracks.

Dawn was breaking behind me, and I realized it was time for me to look for a place to conceal myself during the daylight hours. I was pleased with my performance so far, estimating that I had covered at least ten miles that night. I had no idea how far I would have to walk to reach Luxembourg, or know I had arrived when I got there, but I guessed it would take a few nights to make the journey.

At the first opportunity, I left the track to follow a lane leading to what appeared to be a fairly large wooded area. By this time I was completely exhausted, and perhaps less alert than I should have been as I once again walked into trouble. It was still dark as I rounded a bend in the lane, to come face to face with a dozen or so civilian workers chatting amongst themselves. As I was almost on top of them, I decided to bluff things out this time rather than turn on my heels and run. I veered over to the far side of the road from them to saunter past, trying to appear as casual as I could wearing an Irvin jacket and flying boots, and praying that I should not be recognized as an alien in the early morning twilight. As we passed I was, surprisingly, greeted with a chorus of 'guten Morgens' and was about to congratulate myself on surmounting yet another hurdle, when I heard the word 'Halt' in a high and authoritative voice.

I immediately broke into a sprint. There was a loud report of a pistol shot. I stopped in my tracks. To be shot at from afar can be a rather stressful experience but to be shot at from close quarters is positively terrifying. The next shot could find its target.

Raising my arms above my head in reluctant surrender, I turned slowly to face the trigger-happy gunman. A man brandishing a Luger pistol had detached himself from the group and was standing no more than twenty feet away from me. He was a short, medium built person, with a round face and a Charlie Chaplin moustache. He was wearing steel-rimmed spectacles and the black uniform of a factory security guard – a *Werksschutzpolizei*. He was standing propped against a bicycle that was far too big for him. He was a Heinrich Himmler lookalike, a nasty straight out of a wartime propaganda film about the Gestapo.

As I walked over to him, he nervously backed off and, in doing so, clumsily toppled back over the cycle. This immediately brought a few loud chortles from the group of labourers who were now taking a passive interest in the proceedings. Despite Heinrich's amusing antics as he wrestled to regain his feet, he somehow managed to keep the Luger pointing threateningly at me.

When he did get to his feet he was in quite a paddy. Thrusting the cycle into my hands, he then swaggered about the lane proclaiming his hatred for *Engländer* in general and *Terrorfliegers* in particular: emphasizing his disapproval by taking running kicks at me. The cycle served to protect my shins. Now I was a *Terrorflieger*.

After he had sent what appeared to be a forced labour party on their way, I was escorted to a cottage standing a short distance away in the village. It was a picture postcard cottage detached from a number of equally quaint homes.

As soon as we entered this living room Heinrich's attitude towards me took a change for the better – almost benign. Indicating a chair well away from the doors, he invited me to sit at a table that seemed to fill the room. From the foot of the stairs he called to his family to arouse themselves and to come down to see the *Engländer flieger* he had captured. Heinrich then made excited telephone calls. He was a hero of the Third Reich and would have something to talk about for the rest of his life.

The room was well furnished with a cooking range dominating one side: a log fire was just beginning to take hold in the grate. On the mantelpiece there was a large carved clock and framed photographs. On the walls were portraits of the Nazi hierarchy, the most prominent being Adolf Hitler – with his Charlie Chaplin moustache.

Soon two young girls, neither more than ten years of age, appeared at the foot of the stairs. They were two pretty children, who coyly appraised the fairly good looking *Engländer* aviator sitting in their living room. There was no animosity shown, just curiosity. I smiled, they giggled. When their mother appeared, she just gave me a scornful look and attended to the stove. She and Heinrich then carried on a conversation that lasted for some minutes. I did not understand a word of it, but I guessed it was being explained in detail how I was captured, no doubt with total disregard for his own safety. His family were very impressed.

In an obvious attempt to be as hospitable as possible under all the circumstances, Heinrich let me have a look at the family photograph album. There were the usual wedding photographs, snaps of the children at varying ages, and a sepia photograph of dad in the Kaiser's Army. As the fraternizing continued, I proudly showed them the photograph of Joyce in her Land Army uniform. As we were getting on so well, I thought it the right thing to do.

It was far more satisfying than being questioned by the Gestapo. However, that experience was yet to come.

I was treated to a cup of acorn coffee and some black bread with pork dripping, which I soon disposed of. Heinrich then handed me a piece of paper and a pencil to record my name and number.

After about ninety minutes, two police officers appeared in the doorway. The grey-green Gendarmerie uniforms with brown piping added a splash of colour against the drab black uniform worn by my captor. One of the officers was so tall that he had to remove his inverted coal scuttle shaped helmet to duck under the door frame. The other one was short and fat. The fat one stared at me and loosened his pistol in its holster, conveying the impression that he was quick on the draw and to try to escape would be extremely foolish. As professional police officers, taking a man into custody, regardless of his crime or nationality or performing escort duty was all in a day's work to them. It was not like that with Heinrich. As soon as the officers entered the room he started up again, adopting an officious and aggressive manner towards me – even though I was sure it was pure bravado on his part.

The officers must have congratulated Heinrich on his capture. His chest expanded and from the look on his face he expected no less than a personal visit from the Führer to be decorated with the Iron Cross – First Class.

As I was led to a waiting car with a civilian driver, I reflected that I still did not know Heinrich's real name or whether he intended to warn me or do me grievous bodily harm when he fired the pistol in the lane. Having been in his company for a while, I would not have been entirely surprised if he had pulled the trigger by accident. I consoled myself that I could have fallen into the hands of someone far more dangerous to my health than Heinrich.

It was broad daylight when we set off in the car, which I assumed had been commandeered for the occasion. The tall police officer sat beside me on the back seat, while his colleague kept the driver company. My companion chatted away sociably in fluent English. In fact, he talked incessantly. He informed me that I was captured five miles south-west of Trier, and only a mile from the Luxembourg border. I would have needed another couple of hours

54

1. The author, Tony Johnson, and his wife, Joyce, following their wedding on 19 May 1945.

(*Tony Johnson*)

2. A view of East Vince Moor Farm at Croft-on-Tees, taken from an aircraft dispersal point.
(via Tony Johnson)

3. The crew of Wellington 'G for George'. The photo was taken with a Brownie camera a few days before they were shot down. L to R, rear gunner Bill Ostaficiuk, wireless operator/air gunner Tony Johnson, pilot Steve Tomyn, bomb aimer Bert Symons and navigator Geoff Hall.
(via Tony Johnson)

4. Wellington aircraft of 420 (Snowy Owl) Squadron at Middleton-St-George, Durham, the most northerly airfield in No.6 Group, Royal Canadian Air Force.

(Canadian Forces Photographic Unit, Ottawa)

5. 427 (Lion) Squadron badge showing King George VI's approval.

(Canadian Forces Photographic Unit, Ottawa)

6. The IG Farben chemical works at Oppau, Ludwigshafen, showing heavy bomb
damage and craters. *(Canadian Forces Photographic Unit, Ottawa)*

7. Gutted buildings in the residential area of Mannheim.
(Canadian Forces Photographic Unit, Ottawa)

to reach the border with France. That little gem of information did nothing to lift me from the doldrums. I felt like bursting into tears.

I was being taken to a police station on the outskirts of Trier to await the arrival of a Luftwaffe escort which was coming from an airfield near Bonn.

He went on to prophesy that it was most unlikely that I would be a prisoner of war for long and would soon be on my way home. This was because the Fatherland would soon be victorious: apart from a couple of setbacks at El Alamein and Stalingrad, the glorious Wehrmacht had performed remarkably well in the present conflict. The Allies could not win, and there was no alternative but to sue for peace. He loathed war, and yearned for the time when foreign tourists could be welcomed back to Germany to enjoy the beautiful scenery and quality wines to be found only in the Moselle and Rhine Valleys.

He was obviously a very direct and patriotic person but, nevertheless, a most amiable and sociable one. Perhaps too friendly. I was wary of becoming involved in a dialogue with him for fear of falling into a large trap set by a shrewd interrogator. However, I did try to elicit some information about my aircraft and the fate of the rest of the crew. They had heard of two bombers being shot down in the region overnight, but as they had not been on duty long they could not elaborate. They had been too busy coming to collect me.

I turned my attention to the passing countryside. It was pleasantly undulating scenery, although I was in no frame of mind to appreciate it. I was interested in the style of architecture and the orderliness of the villages we passed through. There was no sign that the country was at war here. However, in the built up areas it was so different. A thought passed my mind that there must have been a flourishing flag making industry in the Reich to satisfy the demand for swastikas. These red, white and black symbols of Nazi tyranny adorned the residential, office, factory and municipal buildings everywhere. Unless it was deemed compulsory to fly these flags, I could only believe that Hitler and his cronies had the total support of the population – at least in this part of the Reich.

Soon after entering the southern outskirts of Trier, we pulled up at a Roman Catholic convent. The driver was dismissed and I was taken into the building. It was obvious that the officers were on cordial terms with the Mother Superior and her brood of nuns. So far as they were able to give me, I received first class treatment. They were indeed angels of mercy as I was given facilities to wash and shave, and what a relief it was to use the strangely shaped and plumbed water closet. I was feeling a lot more refreshed as I tucked into a piece of bread and marmalade, and a cup of coffee. After no more than thirty minutes it was time to leave. I thanked the sisters for their most gracious hospitality – and signed the visitors book. It was a memorable experience.

Walking along the pavement in my RAF flying gear, and sand-wiched between two policemen, I was bound to attract the attention of those passers-by who recognized me as the enemy. These people expressed their hatred for what I stood for by shaking their fists and snarling the words I was so often to hear in the coming months: *Terrorflieger* and *Luftgangster*. Those who ventured close to throw a punch or to kick at me, were firmly turned aside by my escorts cum minders. Whilst their actions were understandable, I resented being subjected to their insults and abuse without being able to retaliate. This was not the time to remind them of the Blitz, of Coventry or Brentwood.

We walked the gauntlet of those incensed Germans for about fifteen minutes before arriving at a police sub-office. It was a prefabricated cabin, likely replacing a bombed out police station – although I did not pursue this possibility. My escorts had behaved impeccably and I was not going to sour our relationship.

The office was sparsely furnished with a desk, two chairs and a filing cabinet. There was a telephone, a typewriter and several shelves and a portrait of Adolf Hitler, in Agfa-colour.

A kettle was put on a gas ring to boil, but not for a cup of tea. While one officer shaved, the other had me turning out my pockets on to the desk. My few belongings comprised two packets of twenty cigarettes, a Ronson lighter, a few Horlicks tablets, a sixpenny piece, and a small portrait of Joyce in her Land Army uniform. These were itemized and placed in a manilla envelope taken down from one of the shelves, except for the cigarettes and

56

lighter which were returned to me. The wristwatch was over-looked.

As a gesture of my appreciation for the way I had been treated, I gave them a packet of cigarettes to share as a token of goodwill. The officers were most appreciative and were soon indulging themselves with Canadian cigarettes. Although I was not going to perform any heroics, it was noticeable that they never once dropped their guard; the Luger was always within their reach and out of mine.

I soon dozed off, but not for long. I was awakened by someone violently shaking me, and standing over me was a character of medium build who looked like a cross between Robin Hood and a deerstalker. The man from the Gestapo wore a fetching green jacket and trousers made of tweed material, socks and brown boots. He was certainly not the stereotype Gestapo person portrayed by film stars in the American propaganda films of the past few years. He reeked of perfume, and even his Tyrolean hat, complete with a feather, was green. He demanded to know my personal particulars, and I gave him my name, rank and number. He then questioned me at length as to the whereabouts of my escape money. I could not convince him that I had not been issued with French and German currency and he became quite cross and shouted that I was a liar. As he was getting nowhere with me, he turned his attention to the two police officers. He apparently accused them of misappropriating the money and a heated argument ensued. However, with the odds of two to one, he soon backed down, confiscating my Irvin jacket as a consolation prize. The two police officers had undoubtedly experienced arrogant Gestapo agents before, standing their ground and afterwards treating the whole episode with indifference although, at the same time, reluctant to become involved in the rights and wrongs of dealing with POW property and the Gestapo.

I was left to my thoughts while the officers dealt with some administration work. Pondering the events of the previous twelve hours, I considered myself extremely fortunate in still being alive. I prayed that the rest of my crew had survived, and had better luck than I had in evading capture. The correspondence under my pillow at Croft would have been found by now, and probably put in the post by the squadron padre. I wondered how the sprog crew in our billet would feel when we failed to show, and I guessed our beds were getting new sheets ready for another sprog crew. I was going to miss Joyce's company so very much.

I soon nodded off to sleep again.

Chapter 5

STEVE IS KILLED

During the early afternoon I awoke to find two young Luftwaffe airmen crowded in the confined space of the office – one a sergeant and the other a corporal. Both had sidearms, but the Sergeant was also carrying a sub-machine gun slung over one shoulder. After a few minutes chat with the police officers, my new escort signed for my property and led me to a camouflaged canvas-covered lorry.

While the Corporal climbed into the driver's cab, the Sergeant steered me through a few bystanders who had gathered at the back of the lorry.

As I climbed onto the tailboard, I realized that the object of interest was a bundled parachute and harness, from which a brown suede flying boot was protruding. I guessed instinctively that one of my crew was under the shroud of silk. There was an expression of sadness as the Sergeant drew his hand across this throat and said quietly: 'Tot! Kaput!', confirming my worse fears. I gently pulled back the canopy, to reveal the lifeless face of Steve Tomyn. I recoiled in horror and felt a bit queasy. Steve would not be keeping the wedding date with Connie – ever! The quiet gentleman from Two Hills, Alberta, had sacrificed his life in saving his crew. Sadly, one of the hazards of being a bomber pilot in a crashing aircraft was that, in satisfying himself that all his crew had baled out, it was often too late to save his own life due to being too near to the ground. Poor Steve! And poor Connie at Leamington Spa.

In my despair, I reproached the onlookers for gawping in

59

morbid curiosity into the back of the lorry. They were dispersed by the two police officers: the tall one expressing his sorrow as he wished me *Auf Wiedersehen*.

As we drove towards the town centre of Trier, the Luftwaffe sergeant, by brilliant miming, managed to convey to me the fact that Steve's dead body had been found in a field a few hundred yards from a bomber that had burnt itself out. His parachute had been deployed. No other bodies were found. It was subsequently established that our Wellington crashed in a field on the outskirts of the village of Kirf. We were on our way to pick up another *Engländer flieger*.

It all seemed a terrible nightmare. Before and during my RAF service I had looked upon many dead bodies; unfortunates who had been killed in an air raid; people who had come to grief in flying accidents; and even an airframe fitter who walked into the spinning propeller of an aircraft warming up. None of these incidents had been so harrowing as finding Steve's body in the back of a lorry.

Our next stop was at a mortuary. Steve's body was placed on a wheeled stretcher and taken into the sombre looking building. Within a few minutes we were on our way again.

About thirty minutes later we pulled up at a large municipal building, which appeared some way from the city centre. The Corporal went into the building, and reappeared shortly afterwards in company with a most miserable looking Bill Ostaficiuk. The mere sight of my lanky rear-gunner helped to brighten my day – just a little bit! At least two of us were still alive!

Bill and I sat in the back of the lorry, with Steve's parachute stowed in one corner. We were able to carry on a whispered conversation – drowned by the noise of the lorry – without making it too obvious that we were part of the same crew. It was difficult for Bill to take in the fact that our pilot was dead. As a fellow Canadian he took the news badly – lapsing into stony-faced silence that was to last until we got to a POW camp over a week later.

We travelled in a north-easterly direction for two to three hours through rolling picturesque countryside, to arrive at an airfield during the late afternoon. Bill and I were taken into the guardroom and placed in a cell. While the Sergeant used a telephone on the switchboard, we took it in turns to use the toilet. The view from a window was enough to identify the airfield as a nightfighter base, equipped with matt black coloured Junkers Ju88 aircraft which were sporting optional extras in the form of Lichtenstein air-to-air radar antennae sprouting from their nose cones. A number of these aircraft were dispersed about the airfield, busily being attended by their ground crews. I wondered if one of the Ju88s was the instrument responsible for the plight we were in.

We were taken to a canteen and provided with the first substantial meal in captivity, and we ate it in complete silence, immersed in our thoughts. I toyed with the idea of asking Bill what he had done with my torch which I had handed to him immediately before I baled out, but wisely decided that it was not the time to jeopardize our friendship.

After the meal I left Bill and was escorted across a parade ground to a single-storied administrative block. We passed through a number of offices containing an inquisitive, although non-hostile, staff of young Luftwaffe clerks and teleprinter operators of both sexes. I was then ushered into a large, well furnished office. There were high wing-backed leather chairs and a heavy glass topped table which took up the centre of the room. The glass covered an air operations map of north-west Europe. There were a number of portraits adorning the walls, mostly landscapes, and there was a large one of General of Nightfighters, Joseph Kammhuber, in a place of prominence near the Führer. There was a strong but not unpleasant aroma in the room.

Standing beaming behind the table were three officers, one in his early thirties and the other two not a lot older than myself. They looked immaculate in their blue/grey pilots' uniforms, set off with silver braid piping. The senior officer introduced himself as a major somebody or other, and the other two were *Leutnants*, I believe. The Major spoke impeccable English which, he said, he perfected while working in London before the war.

The Sergeant placed the envelope containing my property on the table. After I had confirmed my name rank and number, the envelope was opened by the Major and the contents emptied out.

Everything that had been put in the envelope at the police office was there, but in addition there was a halfplate size coloured photograph of the Führer looking as arrogant as ever. There was an awkward silence as the five of us stared in amazement at photographs of Herr Adolf Hitler and Miss Joyce Felton lying together on the table: the Germans trying to comprehend why I should want to carry a picture of their beloved Führer, and me wondering who the bloody joker was. I quickly explained that the prettier of the two photographs belonged to me, and the other one was obviously in the envelope when it was taken from the shelf in the police office. This incident was taken lightheartedly by the Germans, as all could see the funny side of it. Consequently, the rest of the interview seemed to be conducted in a less formal manner. I felt more at ease in their company – although I was still wary of pitfalls.

It was explained that the war was over for me, and there would be no more flying until the end of hostilities. With some obvious satisfaction, the major informed me that the Luftwaffe had accounted for no less than thirty-six of our planes during the previous night. At this rate Bomber Command would soon be ineffective and pose little threat to the Fatherland. Many of my comrades had perished. I was sure that one aircraft had been destroyed and, although there were bound to be more, it was most unlikely that thirty-six had been lost. The Germans were exaggerating!

Then came the questions from the Major, prompted now and then by the *Leutnants*. The first was obviously a trick question: How did I like the Halifax? What squadron did I belong to? In which group was it? What was my CO's name? What were the names of the other members of my crew? . . . and so on. To all the questions I simply shrugged my shoulders or shook my head. There was certainly no coercion on their part to make me talk. They were not trained interrogators and seemed quite prepared to leave the job to those who were.

I would be staying on the airfield overnight and would be given a bed in the sick bay. Next day I would be travelling to the main Luftwaffe interrogation centre near Frankfurt-am-Main.

After finishing my coffee and handshakes all round, it was time for the interview to come to an end. Before leaving the room, I asked the Major what would happen to the dead airman I saw in the lorry. After a short conversation with the Sergeant, he expressed sympathy that one of my countrymen was dead and said that the International Red Cross would be informed through the Swiss Legation in Berlin. The dead airman would receive a full military funeral.

After Bill had been interviewed it was late evening and we were ready for bed – we had not had any real sleep for at least thirty hours. We were physically and mentally exhausted. It was some consolation to jump into comfortable beds in an otherwise un-occupied ward in the sick bay. There was an armed guard sitting just inside the door in case we attempted to escape.

We were about the close our eyes, when the ward was invaded by three pilots who unceremoniously planted themselves on our two beds. They were good-humoured lads of our age, who had come for a chat with the enemy *Gefangenen* – prisoners. They were wearing white dress tunics which, at first sight, gave me the impression that they were ward orderlies. In English we could just about understand, they virtually repeated the same questions put to me earlier by their commanding officer. As we yawned and ignored them, they soon realized that they were wasting their time and left; but not before they gave the latest figure of forty aircraft shot down by the Luftwaffe during the night.

It was most likely that they had gone to warm up their Ju88s in preparation for the night's sorties, but we were thankful to see the back of the boisterous, yet undoubtedly gallant, pilots. Once again, I could not help but wonder whether it was one of those lads who had disabled our Wellington.

I dropped off to sleep with a background noise of Junkers Jumo engines warming up. I slept like a log until early the following morning – Sunday 18 April.

As soon as we had finished breakfast, we were driven to Bonn railway station. We were accompanied by the two escorts who had collected us from Trier, and they were going to take us as far as Frankfurt. At the railway station we were rushed into the Provost

Marshal's office situated in the main booking hall. There were a number of military policemen in the office, and I was intrigued by the silver metal breastplate they wore to distinguish them from other ranks.

We were solemnly warned that Cologne was a short distance away and, particularly since the terrible 1,000 bomber raid on that city less than a year before, the feelings of the civilian population against Allied airmen were still running high. People had been known to take the law into their own hands and lynch, or murder by other equally drastic means, airmen who had literally dropped into their hands. A crowded railway station was a very dangerous place for an Allied airman to be. Bill and I heartily endorsed the decision to let us enjoy the sanctuary of the Provost Marshal's office until the arrival of our train.

We managed to board the train to Frankfurt without incident, although it seemed that there was standing room only. Giving the excuse that prisoners were less likely to make an attempt to escape if seated and hemmed in by their guards, four middle-aged civilian women were summarily ejected from their seats by our escort. They very reluctantly changed places with us to stand in the centre aisle. From the heated argument that ensued between the aggrieved women and the Sergeant, coupled with hostile gestures in our direction, they were far from amused at having to vacate their seats for a couple of *Terrorfliegers*. I found the situation most embarrassing – and I could not see such a thing happening on the LNER, LMS or GWR.

The journey to Frankfurt-am-Main took us along the banks of the river Rhine for most of the way, with long stops in the sidings at main stations like Koblenz and Mainz, before arriving at our destination around midday. The journey seemed endless in the crowded and hostile environment of a stuffy railway carriage. Bill and I avoided eye contact with the other passengers as much as possible by gazing out of the windows; the ever changing scenery and the bustling river traffic occupying our attention.

There were spectacular views round every bend in the track, and the pretty riverside villages were colourfully enhanced by a myriad of swastika flags. Perched high on the sides of the valley were

Disney-like fairyland castles, although Germany was by no means a fairyland. It was a giant war machine running in top gear, and the railways were its main arteries linking the battle fronts – particularly the Eastern Front. As soon as we had been shunted into a siding, a troop train would roar past with its carriages packed with military personnel and the flat wagons loaded with tanks and other armaments. Hospital trains would rush by in the opposite direction, carrying the dead and wounded. Some carriages displayed the white cross on the roof. The urgency of these trains seemed to typify Germany's conduct of the war. In my experience the pace was rather less hectic back home. I was rather surprised that, unlike in Blighty, the street names and other informative signs had not been obliterated or removed. It was apparent that Germany was under the mistaken impression that it would soon be victorious, and certainly not be invaded.

Frankfurt railway station was considered to be one of the largest termini in Europe, and I searched in vain to see some bomb damage as our train approached it; nor was there any visible damage to the station or the city itself so far as could be seen. I was disheartened because I fully expected to see areas of devastation, especially as the city had received a visit from Bomber Command about a week before.

Joining the concourse of travellers, both civilian and military, we were hustled through the ticket barrier and into the Provost Marshal's office. We were in the office only long enough for our escort to be replaced by an *Unteroffizier* and a *Gefreiter*. These two Luftwaffe NCOs were mean looking characters who were quite menacing; the *Unteroffizier* resembled a gorilla in uniform who cradled a sub-machine gun. I formed the opinion that these two were bully boys who would do us harm at the slightest provocation.

As we were ushered out of the station and into the street, we were almost immediately surrounded by a mob of snarling and fist-shaking *Herrenvolk* who seemed to have been waiting in ambush. Although we were not completely surprised, we were stunned by the ferocity of the attack. We were at the mercy of a lynch mob and it was most unnerving, made more so by the fact

65

that our escort had stepped aside to let the incensed 'Frankfurters' get on with what they were doing. Bill and I had to make a tactical retreat to get our backs to the nearest wall, and to parry as many of the blows as possible. Intent on murder or inflicting other grievous bodily harm, the mob rained blows on us, they kicked, and spat. We were, among other things, *Schweine* and *Terror-fliegers*. As we seemed unpopular with the locals, we were more than thankful with the arrival of the military police from the Provost Marshal's Office who efficiently dispersed the trouble makers, and then had a shouting match with our escort.

Apart from one or two bruises we came out of the mêlée more shaken than hurt. The most revolting aspect was having to wipe the spittle from our battledress while waiting for a tram to take us for a few miles to Oberürsal, which was situated on the northern outskirts of the city.

Irrespective of the number of uniforms and swastikas in evidence, Frankfurt still retained the appearance of a thriving and popular tourist resort. There were ice cream vendors, bustling department stores, and women sporting spring fashions. No food queues were apparent, and it was difficult to believe that this was a country in its fourth year of war. There was not a bombed-out building or a bomb crater in sight – despite repeated bombing. It was all so depressing and demoralizing. I was far from enthusiastic with the way my war was progressing.

We had to stand on the tram but, thankfully, had to suffer only the contemptuous stares of the other passengers. As the tram trundled slowly towards the suburbs of the city, we were able to see heavy bomb damage to tenement buildings, with workmen busily clearing the rubble and shoring up. Bill and I were now getting cute, and did not cheer or show any sign of noticing the devastation to this part of the Fatherland.

On alighting from the tram at Oberürsal we had a short walk to Dulag-Luft. There were few pedestrians to be seen, and those that were about walked past us without a second look. No doubt the sight of captured Allied airmen making for the prison camp must have been a common occurrence at Oberürsal – almost a daily one.

As we were manhandled past the guard at the main gate of the camp and into the barbed-wire surrounded compound, the truth that I had lost my liberty really came home to me. To escape from one of these top security cages was going to be extremely difficult, but the occasion might present itself sometime.

We were led into a large cheerless concrete and brick building. In one room we were ordered to strip and, standing naked with our feet apart, we had to bend and try to touch our toes and hold that position while we suffered the embarrassment of having our rectums prodded by a medic of the glorious Luftwaffe. A nineteen-year-old can do without that sort of treatment to find out whether he had a secret bomb-sight or whatever stashed away. I felt like telling the prodder that, even if I had been issued with escape money I would not have chosen to stuff it up my backside to keep it from falling into enemy hands.

After dressing, Bill and I were parted. I was taken along a dimly lit corridor flanked by cells until we came to one that was vacant. This was to be my place of confinement and interrogation for the next week. Before the guard closed and locked the thick door of the cell, a door more common to cold storage plants, he explained how I could summon a guard if absolutely necessary. By pulling a knob beside the door inside the cell, a hinged clapper situated on the wall in the corridor would drop with a clatter from the vertical to the horizontal. A guard either hearing the clatter or seeing the clapper sticking out from the wall would open the door, usually to be escorted to the toilet at the end of the corridor. Under no circumstances would I use this 'Heath Robinson' system of communication frivolously, or it would be put out of action indefinitely, and with a diet of sauerkraut and potato soup, a breakdown in communication could have disastrous consequences for a foolish prisoner disobeying this piece of sound advice.

The cell appeared watertight and measured ten by six feet, with a high ceiling, from which was hung a low wattage light bulb. The only furniture was a wooden bed fixed to the wall. Folded on the bed was a sparsely filled straw palliasse and bolster. There were also two blankets that reeked of body odour and which had not been cleaned for months.

There was a small fixed and barred window high in the wall opposite the door, with a dust choked ventilator beside it.

During the week to follow, when not being subjected to interrogation, I would sit on the bed and contemplate my future as a POW. From all the evidence I had seen, there was a long way to go before we bombed the German people into submission and I did not look forward to the prospect of an interminable number of years in captivity. Of course we would win – and soon, I kept reminding myself.

I noticed some brown splash marks on the wall in front of me and I convinced myself that they were dried bloodstains, although whether caused by some uncooperative prisoner being thoroughly beaten up or by a common or garden smack on the nose it was difficult to say. I wondered about instruments of torture. I disliked pain.

Whatever the Germans had in store for me, I took some consolation in the knowledge that, with the invaluable assistance of Bomber Command, I had accomplished to some extent what I had set out to do at the height of the Battle of Britain in 1940.

I was then a seventeen-year-old residing alone in lodgings at Brentwood in Essex. One afternoon while I was driving an Austin Seven van in Kings Road towards the railway station, I became aware that shoppers were behaving oddly by running and diving for cover in shop doorways. I stopped the van and, above the sound of the engine ticking over, I heard the staccato sound of machine guns being fired. I ducked behind the van as bullets whined and ricocheted about the street.

I looked up as the road was overshadowed by the ominous shape of a Dornier Do 17 bomber with the German marking clearly visible in the sunlight. It flew over Kings Road at rooftop level with its front and underside guns blazing away at everything in sight. I kept the aircraft in view as it banked over the railway goods yard and straddled it with a stick of four bombs. Three bombs missed a gasometer but made a mess of the sidings, while the fourth bomb scored a direct hit on the station booking hall.

I was one of the first to reach the scene of devastation. A cloud of dust was settling where the booking office had been only minutes before. The two male ticket clerks had been killed instantly, and their naked dust covered bodies could be seen lying amongst the debris. I had known both by sight but was unable to recognize them without difficulty as they lay lifeless in the rubble.

I was appalled by the suddenness of the attack and the unnecessary death of innocent civilians on a beautiful summer's day. As I waited on the railway bridge for the arrival of the ambulance and rescue services, I vowed to avenge the senseless waste of life and destruction caused that day. I was young and guileless.

Warley Barracks, the home of the Essex Regiment, was situated less than a mile south of Brentwood railway station. From the air it could not be mistaken for anything other than a military establishment with its parade grounds and numerous barrack blocks, and yet it was ignored by the Luftwaffe in the belief, possibly, that the destruction of a station on the LNER Liverpool Street to Southend line was more important to their invasion plans; particularly as it had been bombed unsuccessfully once before.

Although I had completed only three operations – a leaflet raid over France while at OTU, the raid on Duisburg, and the unfortunate raid on Ludwigshafen – I would have to be content with those for the time being. I was so isolated in the cell, and on one of those too rare occasions I turned to God for comfort and guidance. I prayed . . . I prayed that my parents and Joyce would not have too long to wait before they were notified that I was alive in captivity. I prayed that I would have the courage to withstand illtreatment from my captors. I dozed off.

*　　*　　*

Back in England the results of the Friday night's raids were being collated at Bomber Command HQ. Of the 327 sorties to Pilsen, thirty-six aircraft were reported missing (eleven per cent) and of the 270 sorties – one aircraft failed to take off – to Mannheim and Ludwigshafen, eighteen aircraft failed to return (six point six per cent). Subject to any survivors from ditched aircraft being rescued from the North Sea or English Channel, at least 360 aircrew were dead or missing – this represented sufficient manpower to put three bomber squadrons in the air. Of the 360, around 300 would be killed, while the rest would become POWs.

Out of the ninety-one aircraft committed by 6 Group RCAF to the targets, nine failed to return (nine point nine per cent). 408 (Goose) Squadron based at Linton-on-Ouse was decimated. Four of the twelve Halifaxes it dispatched to Pilsen failed to return – a real morale dampener. 420 (Snowy Owl), 425 (Alouette), 429 (Bison) and our squadron, each lost a Wellington aircraft and its crew.

These losses were the highest Bomber Command had suffered in the war up to that date, and from then on only on very rare occasions were two major targets attacked on the same night.

The squadron adjutants would have the unpleasant duty of sending off letters of condolence to the next of kin of the missing, to follow up the telegrams that would have already been wired after all hope had gone.

The raid on Pilsen was a disappointing show. The usually accurate Pathfinder Force had made an unaccountable error by dropping the TIs on a mental asylum some miles short of the Skoda works. There were unconfirmed reports that a few hundred soldiers were killed when their barracks near the asylum was hit by bombs, although it is doubtful whether this improved 'Bomber' Harris' mood, particularly as the Skoda works remained unscathed.

The Mannheim/Ludwigshafen targets were accurately marked by the Pathfinders and widespread destruction was caused to both the industrial and residential areas, coupled with a heavy loss of life to the civilian population. The Farben factory received a number of direct hits and production halted. The raid was considered to be a very successful one.

In view of the fact that I failed to keep the date with Joyce, on the Sunday she decided to cycle over to Croft from Darlington to find out the reason. As she cycled to the guardroom at the main entrance to the airfield, she spotted our normal aircraft at its dispersal near the perimeter fence. Unless I had a reasonable excuse for standing her up, I was going to get a piece of her

70

Geordie mind. I had a reasonable excuse, as she was soon to discover.

She waited at the guardroom while an MP made enquiries of aircrew watching a football match on the sports field. He returned to give her the news that my aircraft was missing on operations. She was in a state of shock as she rode back to the Land Army hostel.

Chapter 6

INTERROGATION AT DULAG-LUFT

Early the following morning I was awakened by the guard as he opened the door. He handed me a razor, towel and a piece of soap, and then accompanied me to the latrine at one end of the corridor. I was warned not to waste too much time as there were many more of my comrades waiting to use the washing facilities. The soap would not lather and had the consistency of clay: however, I felt considerably refreshed after the shave.

After handing back the toiletries, such as they were, I was put back in my cell. The breakfast comprised of a slice of bread spread with ersatz margarine and jam, and a mug of mint tea. The margarine seemed to have been made with the same ingredients as the soap, and the jam was fruit flavoured swede purée. Although I ate the bread and jam, I refused to drink the tea for fear it contained a drug to make me more amenable to interrogation.

Like most of the staff at Dulag-Luft, the guard had a working knowledge of English. In high spirits he remarked that he had never experienced such an influx of my comrades after an overnight raid on the Reich. It was a fact, he said, that the Luftwaffe had accounted for no less than fifty Allied aircraft during Friday night.

Still very sceptical of the German claims and, as the guard appeared a reasonable creature, I made it obvious to him that I thought he was talking a load of nonsense, emphasizing my point by giving him a two-fingered Churchill salute. He became quite cross and obviously considered that such insolence had to be immediately discouraged. Pressing his face close to mine, he snarled a warning that it was most unwise to incur his displeasure at any time, and that it would be in my interest to respect and cooperate fully with any Luftwaffe personnel who visited my cell. I was pleased that he did not splatter my blood about the cell, but instead he drew his Luger and, holding the muzzle close to my face, he queried whether I fully understood him. I told him that he could not have made the position plainer, and secretly promised myself that I would make every effort, within reason, to maintain a more amiable understanding between us for the duration of my stay.

He left the cell, slamming the door shut so hard that the shock waves popped my ears again.

In the absence of a radio or any reading matter, I occupied my time trapping the various specimens of creepy-crawlies also sharing my billet. I slaughtered the more repulsive looking bugs, keeping the more intelligent ones which, I hoped, would respond to training. I was busy examining my catch, dropping the bugs I intended to keep, when the door was opened and a well dressed gentleman came into the cell.

He cheerily wished me a good morning and sat down on the bed beside me. The guard collected my plate and mug, walking off with my entire collection of best bugs. Resting his briefcase on his lap and looking for all the world as though he was about to try and sell me some life insurance, he offered me a cigarette from a freshly opened packet of Players Medium Navy Cut. We then lit up from a lighter which he made sure I recognized as a Ronson. The stage was set.

He benevolently introduced himself as a representative of the International Committee of the Red Cross at Geneva. He was interested to know how I had been treated by the Germans since my capture and had I any cause for complaint? I pointed out some swellings on my face and mentioned the incident at the railway station. He expressed his sympathy but explained that the conduct of the civilian population, whilst most deplorable, was a civil matter and beyond the control of the military. He would make a note of my complaint.

He then advised me that I would be humanely treated as

73

Germany fully abided by the rules of the Geneva Convention. He looked forward to the end of the war so that all prisoners of war could be reunited with their families, and so on.

Not only was he a charmer, but he smelled as though he had showered in eau de cologne.

He then got down to the nitty-gritty. Only the Red Cross organization would be able to quickly get word to my parents that I was safe and a prisoner of war and it was in my own interest to complete a form for administrative purposes in order that the matter could be quickly dealt with from head office in Geneva.

He proffered another cigarette the moment I stubbed out the first one, and then produced a form of questionnaire from his briefcase. Handing it to me, he advised that I should take my time and answer every question.

The initial questions caused me no concern as I was merely asked to give my name, rank and service number, together with details of my parents and my home address. The second part, however, sought details of my squadron, the names of my commanding officer and the rest of my crew. These questions I refused to answer and I handed back the partly completed form.

I now completely distrusted him and was convinced that he was a German intelligence officer rather than the ICRC representative he purported to be. We had been warned to expect the bogus ICRC agent in such circumstances.

This one persisted. He was insistent that nothing I put on the form would be divulged to the Germans. He also complained that I was wasting his time unnecessarily as there were many more of my comrades to be processed.

After I had chain-smoked four of his cigarettes he finally gave up. Obviously quite vexed, he snatched up the packet of cigarettes and only a locked door prevented him storming out of the cell. While he waited for the guard to let him out, he muttered something about the lack of cooperation, and it was quite possible that my parents would wait months before they heard of my whereabouts.

During the days that followed I had numerous visits from intelligence officers – the Abwehr, but there was nothing secret about their methods of interrogation and they made no bones about the fact that they were there to extract as much information about my service life as possible.

They adopted the 'good guy, bad guy technique' of questioning. Two officers took it in turns to visit the cell and question me, one an outright bully who only just stopped short of physical violence, followed by the other who had only his halo missing. He promised eternal salvation if I gave a complete rundown on my squadron. Although I felt a bit of a prune sitting for hours staring ahead, it would have been fraught with danger to enter into any sort of dialogue, especially with the 'good guy'.

I believe the fact that there were a lot more prisoners in the establishment to be interrogated let me off the hook to some extent. I doubt whether I was subjected to the sort of intensive questioning those before me must have endured.

On my sixth day of confinement, the bogus ICRC representative came into my cell for the last time. On this occasion he made no pretence that he was anything other than an intelligence officer. He was carrying a folder under his arm on which was printed 427 Squadron in bold graphics. He made himself comfortable on the bed, opened the folder and, with an arrogant smirk on his face, he recited a brief history of my squadron, including Christian names and personal family details of senior officers. He finished by assuring me that I was a member of the squadron, and asked if I wished to add anything.

I was far too nonplussed to add anything to his file, even if I was so inclined. He had a large amount of information at his finger tips, even if much of it was pure fabrication of details of which I could have no knowledge. I was simply flabbergasted by the amount of knowledge the Luftwaffe had gleaned of a squadron not yet five months old, and undoubtedly of Bomber Command as a whole.

I sat and wondered just how much intelligence was obtained by Nazi agents and sympathizers operating in the vicinity of the squadrons back home, and just how much was extracted from prisoners by interrogation at Dulag-Luft. I convinced myself that the intimate details of the officers' family lives and backgrounds must come from the Luftwaffe's agents in the UK, while other details would probably be extracted from the completed form handed back to the bogus ICRC representative, who was doubtless one of the more successful interrogators at Dulag-Luft.

After a week on bare rations of black bread, swede jam, and cabbage or swede soup, my stomach was protesting at the change of diet. Consequently, I suffered from a mild form of diarrhoea and this, coupled with a high pressured flatulence, produced a worrying combination. However, before there was a need to repeatedly summon the guard to dash to the latrine, I was taken from the cell for good. My inquisition had come to an end.

I was led into a large communal room where I was delighted to see Bill and Bert standing with about thirty other air force POWs. Still very much aware that the room may be bugged, we carried out a strange, almost whispered conversation to update ourselves with the series of events.

Bert's face was black and blue where his parachute had snagged in a tree and he had slammed into the trunk. He had a difficult time reaching the ground, and was soon captured by a soldier and a particularly nasty Hitler Youth. When he baled out of the aircraft, Steve and Geoff were still to follow.

It was a strange gathering in the room, with airmen standing in groups, furtively glancing over their shoulders before whispering anything they did not want the enemy to pick up. The men in the room were the survivors from so many crews that the Bomber Command's casualty figures must surely have been exceptionally high and gave some credence to the claims made by the Luftwaffe.

We listened intently while a Luftwaffe officer read out names from a list and formed us into small groups. The few aircrew officers were going to Stalag-Luft III in Silesia, while the NCO ranks were bound for Stalag-Luft I, a camp near Barth on the Baltic Coast. He said these were to be our permanent camps for the duration of the war. And we cheered! We cheered not because we were overjoyed at the prospect of being incarcerated for goodness knows how long, but rather because it was the result of the euphoria brought about by mixing with colleagues who, during the past eight days, had experienced the most traumatic times in their lives. We refused to give the enemy the satisfaction of seeing that we were so bloody miserable. For their part, the Germans thought we were completely round the bend.

As I was climbing onto the lorry to take me to Frankfurt railway station, I spotted Geoff with a batch of prisoners entering the camp. I only had time to shout and pass on the sad news about Steve's death before the lorry moved off. For four to survive out of a crew of five was something to be thankful for in view of all the circumstances.

At the railway station I expected a repetition of the fun and games we had to put up with the week before, but nothing materialized. We were shepherded to a carriage waiting at a siding without having to run a gauntlet of bloodthirsty locals. As it was a Sunday perhaps most of them were at church, some even confessing their sins.

Our party was to occupy one carriage and, after the week of solitary confinement and the attention of the Abwehr inquisitors, we behaved like overgrown children on a day's outing, scrambling for the window seats. I scrambled for the seat nearest to the toilet compartment, or the equivalent to an Elsan chemical lavatory.

The guards were getting on in years and claimed they were First World War veterans. The one doing his stint of watching us carefully always nursed the sub-machine gun on his lap. Both conveyed the impression that they would not stand for any nonsense from us, in fact they were just waiting for the opportunity to shoot one of us to set an example. One of them had the task of looking after a large box containing the food rations for the journey.

The carriage had been adapted for the conveyance of prisoners to either prison or concentration camps, and its doors could only be opened from the outside. The windows could not be opened and the small one in the toilet compartment was reinforced with barbed wire.

It was approximately 280 miles from Frankfurt to Barth which was situated on the Baltic coast, and eight miles north of the main Rostock to Stralsund road.

The route we were to take was via Hannover, Schwerin and

Rostock, and then on to Barth. We had to spend one uncomfortable night in the sidings at Schwerin, and at Rostock we were once
again sidetracked while other trains were given priority.

During the night at Schwerin, the guards took it in turns to
watch over us. We were given no opportunity to escape while we
were on the train, although I was treated as a suspect escaper
because of the number of times I used the toilet – at least until I
managed to recover from the problem with my bowels.

One or two of the lads were still in a state of shock following
being suddenly and violently excused flying duties for the duration of the war. We were unable to communicate with one airman
who had suffered a complete mental block. He simply stared into
space with his lifeless eyes, completely devastated. He should have
been receiving hospital treatment rather than travelling to a prison
camp.

The daily food ration comprised an eighth of a loaf of bread,
and about six ounces of liver sausage, per man per day. And no
afters! Flasks of water were replenished by one of the guards when
we stopped at a station. There was no point in complaining about
the quality or quantity of the food because the guards fared no
better.

The train chugged slowly through delightful scenery and past
many picturesque villages. It puzzled me how the inhabitants of a
country with such charm could plunge the world into two wars
within a quarter of a century. I could only conclude that militancy
and expansionism were endemic in the character of the German
nation. I was to learn that barbarism was another trait.

We pulled into Barth station during the afternoon. In common
with the majority of the urban railway stations in Germany, it was
a good walk to the town centre, and Stalag-Luft I was about a mile
away in the other direction.

It was a beautiful day, and we were pleased with the opportunity to stretch our legs following the tiresome journey from
Frankfurt. The terrain was flat and uninteresting – much like the
fens of Cambridgeshire – and the area had been designated a bird
sanctuary, or *Vogelschutzgebeit*. Skylarks and other song birds
were making themselves heard under a clear blue sky, and the sea

breeze coming from the Baltic felt so invigorating. Only the presence of the jackbooted guards and the sight of a Dornier Do 17 with its undercarriage down circling to land, reminded me that I was a long, long way from Canvey Island or Cromer.

As we approached the camp along a narrow cobbled road, we were surprised at the large area it covered compared with what we had been allowed to see of the detention compound at Dulag-Luft. Stalag-Luft I was in the form of a square stockade, with each of its perimeter fences about 300 yards long and eight feet high. These were twin fences, one behind the other, with a gap of six feet. The space between the fences was filled with coiled barbed wire to a height of approximately four feet. At each corner of the camp, and at other strategic positions, there were watch towers on stilts, each with a guard or *Wachposten*, a Schmeisser machine gun and a spotlamp. At intervals of forty yards along the perimeter fences there were floodlights fixed ten feet above the ground. Armed dog handlers patrolled the outside of the camp with Alsatians. Only Alcatraz could have looked more formidable to a sprog POW.

An ill-humoured looking guard opened the gate sufficiently wide enough to let us, reluctantly, file through into the *Vorlager*. The *Vorlager* was that part of the camp that held the Luftwaffe administration offices, the guards' quarters, the sick bay, the food parcel store, the cookhouse, and the detention block – the cooler.

We were greeted with a rousing cheer from a welcoming committee of prisoners lined up behind the single barbed wire fence separating the main *Lager* from the *Vorlager*. It appeared that the whole of the camp's population of just over 300 prisoners had turned out to get to know the latest news from home. There would be some delay while we went through the routine of being searched, documented and allocated a POW number.

First the strip search, and, once again, I had to endure the degrading performance of having to touch my toes while some moron on the staff of the camp Abwehr examined my anus and, for no other reason than to satisfy his depravity, prodded my testicles with a cane.

After I had dressed I joined a queue for my personal property, and witnessed an incident that nearly resulted in our first casualty at Stalag-Luft I. An Abwehr sergeant seated at one of the desks, picked out a photograph from property belonging to an airman standing just ahead of me in the queue. It was a snap of a woman in a swimsuit. The sergeant made some crude remark and then, as though goading the airman into action, he rubbed the photograph in a circular motion against his own crotch. The airman had to be restrained from striking out at the German, who immediately leapt to his feet and drew his Luger. Standing back out of harms way, the sergeant deliberately tore the photograph into pieces. It was an ugly scene, and our first encounter with one of the many guards who thoroughly enjoyed baiting us, in the hope that we would overstep the mark and provide the excuse to maim or kill.

Before leaving the building I was handed an oval aluminium identity disc with *KRIEGSGEFANGENER Nr 1009* stamped on it. I was now a full fledged *Kriegie*.

We crossed the *Vorlager* to the gate giving access to the main *Lager*. As we waited for more prisoners to join us before the guard opened the gate, there was an exchange of friendly banter through the wire. To a question of how long he had been a prisoner, one replied with a broad Australian accent: 'Work it out for yourself, sport . . . Pontius was my Pilate!' Without a trace of a smile, another wanted to know if pneumatic tyres had yet been fitted to Sopwith Camel biplanes. The Germans were not the only ones who found difficulty in fathoming out our sense of humour; humour that came to the fore in adversity.

I was pleased to notice that Bill and Bert were in the group as we entered the main *Lager* and were shown to our living accommodation. Towels, razor, clean underwear, etc, were waiting for us – with the compliments of the Red Cross. However, the cutlery was embossed with the swastika.

Before we got settled in, we paraded in the camp theatre for pep talks by the Camp Leader, the Medical Officer and the Chaplain.

The Camp Leader, or the British Man of Confidence to the Red Cross, was Group Captain J. C. MacDonald. He was a long serving *Kriegie* who began his talk by reminding us that it was a duty to try to escape, but only with the approval of the camp

Escape Committee. Then followed a series of dos and don'ts, with emphasis on the don'ts that could incur the death penalty carried out by a trigger-happy goon guard. He warned us to expect sudden thorough searches by the camp security, or ferrets. The person in charge of security was a staunch Nazi with little sense of humour, one *Hauptmann* von Miller zu Aicholz. He was to be avoided as much as possible, particularly if in the act of escaping. The ferrets were usually getting on in years, and not considered very bright. Nevertheless, even morons could point firearms and pull the triggers. Any fraternizing with a goon should be left to the experts in this field.

The British Medical Officer was Captain Nichols, an army MO captured in 1940. He explained that whilst he was always on call, he had limited medical supplies and sick bay accommodation. He strongly discouraged *Kriegies* attending sick parades with frivolous complaints – like hunger pangs and homesickness.

Finally the Chaplain, the Reverend R. Drake-Brackman, did his utmost to make us feel at home and wanted. He was always available. He would be pleased to see us at his Sunday services. The offertory box had been dispensed with.

These officers, and the Camp Leader's aide, Squadron Leader W. Turner, were the only commissioned *Kriegies* in the camp. With the exception of the Medical Officer, they would soon be transferred to Stalag-Luft III which was in the process of becoming a camp for commissioned ranks only – the equivalent to an Oflag for army officers.

On our return to the barrack block we spent some time updating the senior *Kriegies* with the latest news from home, even if it was a week old. We were also issued with our first Red Cross parcels. All in all, conditions were much better than any of us had visualized. It was explained that the guards were generally referred to as 'goons'. There were exceptions of course, such as 'ferrets', 'jerries', 'krauts' and, depending upon the occasion, there were 'bastards' and 'shithouses'; the use of suitable vulgar adjectives being completely discretionary.

Before we were locked in the barrack blocks for the night, there was time for us to stretch our legs by doing a couple of circuits of

81

the main *Lager*. About thirty feet from the perimeter fence, and a foot from the ground, there was a trip or warning wire. The goons had orders to shoot on sight any *Kriegie* foolish enough to be seen trespassing in the area between the trip wire and the fence. There was no right of appeal, and the goons could show no mercy: they had to obey orders.

There were six barrack blocks in the *Lager*, three of which were used mostly by the British, and the others by Commonwealth and other Allied prisoners, such as the Poles and the Czechs. The barrack blocks were divided into nine rooms, plus a cooking area and a latrine. In view of the fact that the camp was only partially full at that time, the number of double tier bunks in each room varied between six and ten to a room. Each barrack was equipped with two cooking ranges and a number of stoves for heating, incidental cooking and brew-ups.

There was a large communal latrine in the *Lager*, which contained twenty toilet cubicles – minus doors – urine troughs, wash troughs, and cold water showers.

In the adjoining *Lager* which was used as a parade ground and a football field, the only building was the camp theatre.

Although it would take weeks for me to adjust to POW life, or *Kriegsgefangenschaft* as the locals called it, the fact that I was sharing it with the 'cream of British youth' helped a great deal. Many were almost thirty years-of-age, old boys who possessed years of experience of living with the enemy.

Freedom was something always taken for granted, and I now realized just how much it was worth fighting for.

*   *   *

Stalag-Luft I was built and taken into use in late 1942, primarily to take the overflow from Stalag-Luft III and to bring together those airmen who had found themselves in army POW camps. A number of these airmen had exchanged identities with soldiers so that they could join the outside working detachments where there were more opportunities to escape. Thus, we had the company of one or two soldiers who could pass on first-hand experiences of being left behind at Dunkirk, being overrun by Rommel's Afrika Corps in the desert, or fighting a losing battle in Norway. Within a few months, such would be the RAF and American 8th Air Force losses, that Stalag-Lufts I and III were unable to absorb the number of airmen taken prisoner and new camps were soon to be constructed at Heydekrug in East Prussia and Gross Tychow in Pomerania.

The initial intake to Stalag-Luft I amounted to only thirty prisoners and these undoubtedly enjoyed the halcyon days of POW life if, indeed, there were such days of *Kriegsgefangenschaft*. Rumour had it that it was not unusual for parties of *Kriegies* to be escorted to the beach at Barth to spend a few hours sunbathing or swimming. Conditions had certainly deteriorated by the time I arrived at the camp, and instead of a head count of thirty the number had multiplied tenfold.

By midsummer 1943, the population of the camp had grown to 553, with British *Kriegies* accounting for seventy-six per cent, Canadians fifteen per cent, Australasians four per cent, and Rhodesians, Czechs, and Poles making up the balance.

The consistent losses, sustained not only by Bomber Command, but now also by the growing American 8th Air Force, were confirmed by the fact that just prior to our move from Stalag-Luft I in October 1943, its population had increased to over 1,000 prisoners. Despite the losses, there was no let up by the Allied offensive against the Reich which, weather permitting, was being targeted by night and day.

Chapter 7

STAMMLAGER-LUFT I, BARTH

Still rather bemused by what was happening to me, I tried to make an effort to accept the situation and settle into my new surroundings, and so did eleven others who shared the room. The Hut Leader and two other old-timers popped along to introduce themselves and assist in any way they could. It seemed that there were cigarettes galore.

There were spare double-tier bunks in the room, so I managed to get an upper bunk which seemed the most popular. It was near a window and gave me a good all round view of what was happening about me. Each bunk had just enough wooden slats across its width to support a body, although with some discomfort. It was complete with a palliasse, bolster and an army blanket.

The lower bunks were generally preferred by the lame, wounded, the less energetic, those who sought semi-reclusion, and those who suffered with weak bladders. In certain circumstances the lower bunks could be extremely dangerous places, especially after the compulsory removal of slats to provide shoring timber for a well advanced escape tunnel. One false move in the upper bunk would result in either slats being dislodged to thump down to give a sleeping prisoner a rude awakening, or be equally disturbed by the full weight of his bunk mate landing on top of him. These alarming disturbances that always seemed to occur during the middle of the night, caused nerves to fray and most insensitive language to be exchanged; understandably, perhaps, when accidents of this nature could cause serious injury.

84

Before we had been in the room long it began to reek very much like a rugby players' dressing room after the match. This was partly because most outdoor ball games were being played by the 'cream of British and Commonwealth youth' clad only in the clothes they stood in, and also by virtue of the fact that there was seldom any water other than cold and the laundry facilities left a lot to be desired.

The large table in the centre of the room close to the stove was the forum for many debates on how the war should be fought; the chess, monopoly and card games, and occasionally a place to sit down to have a meal. Meals using the contents of Red Cross parcels were prepared by an individual *Kriegie* and a combine of two or more *Kriegies*. There were considerable advantages to be had by joining a combine inasmuch as it provided stricter rationing and the food kept fresh for as long as was required, before opening a can. The loner had to scoff down a tin of pink salmon once he had opened the tin and this was not an economical way of using a food parcel. However, the choice of whether or not to join a combine remained with the individual.

During our stay at Stalag-Luft I there was a regular supply of Red Cross food parcels, resulting in a weekly issue of a parcel per *Kriegie*. They were mainly British parcels, occasionally substituted with American or Canadian. The weight of a parcel was 10lbs and, although the presentation of the North American differed to some extent, they contained the following canned goodies: stewed or pressed meat, pink salmon, cheese, vegetables, powdered and tinned milk, powdered egg and biscuits. There were also prunes, tea, cocoa, chocolate, porridge, soap, vitamin pills and cigarettes. Whatever the source of the parcel the nutritional value was about the same. In addition to the cigarettes contained in the parcels, there was usually a further weekly issue of fifty with the compliments of the Red Cross.

The minimum weekly ration of food provided by the Germans, as stipulated by the Red Cross, was also about 10lbs in weight and ought to have included fat, meat, bread, margarine, cheese, dried vegetables, jam, sugar, barley and potatoes. The combination of the parcels and what the goons condescended to give us, provided a fairly reasonable diet under the circumstances. Most of us found the energy to play outdoor sports, the most popular games were volleyball, football and rugby. The game of softball was favoured by the Canadians, but this was superseded by baseball as the American presence grew in the camp. All the sports equipment, whether new or secondhand was donated by the YMCA and other charitable organizations and delivered to the camp by the Red Cross.

The food provided to us by the goons was prepared by *Kriegies* in the cookhouse situated in the *Vorlager*. To become a cook and commute daily to the cookhouse was one of the most sought after jobs in the camp, but there were seldom vacancies. These cordon bleu *Kriegies* were old-timers who operated a form of closed shop. They took pains to let us know that the fact they looked better fed than the average *Kriegie* was purely coincidental and had nothing to do with their voluntary work to ensure our well-being. Nevertheless, until food came to be a lot harder to come by, they were not begrudged the extra mouthful.

The daily ration of black bread was about an inch thick, and was accompanied by perhaps swede jam or liver sausage to make do for breakfast and tea. The midday meal invariably meant a handful of potatoes boiled in their jackets, with barley or vegetable soup or horsemeat chunks in consommé. Occasionally the goons would surprise us with one-off items, such as a large rusted tin of minced herrings canned in Norway, or a job lot of brie cheese that was well past its best, to be shared among so many *Kriegies*.

Bread and potatoes made up the bulk of the German rations. The potatoes were of a quality rejected for use in pig-swill, but were invariably scoffed with relish in their jackets – there was no waste of food in the camp. Before being cut and distributed, the loaves weighed about 2lb and had the colour and consistency of malt loaf with sawdust as the main ingredient. One soon acquired a taste for the bread which made a tasty snack with cheese topping.

Throughout the day, and sometimes during the night, there would be someone making a snack or brewing up on the stove in the room. Although there was a weekly issue of coal blocks for

ROYAL CANADIAN AIR FORCE
OVERSEAS

No.427 Squadron, R.C.A.F.

April 22, 1943.

Dear Mr.Johnson

    Before you received this letter, you will have had a telegram informing you that your Son, Sergeant Anthony Frederick Johnson, has been reported as missing as a result of air operations.

    It is with regret that I write to you this date, to convey to Anthony's family, the feelings of my entire Squadron. On the night of the 16th April, 1943, at approximately nine o'clock Anthony and his crew took off from this aerodrome to carry out a bombing attack over enemy territory, and were due to return at approximately four o'clock in the morning. Unfortunately, the aircraft never returned and we have heard nothing from it or any member of the crew since time of take-off.

    We lost one of our best crews when this aircraft did not return, for it had already been mapped out for a great future with the Squadron.

    Your Son was very popular with this Squadron and fast becoming an ace Wireless Operator. He is greatly missed in the Sergeants Mess and his loss is felt by all.

    There is always the possibility that your Son may be a prisoner-of-war, in which case you will either hear from him direct or through the Air Ministry, who will receive advice from the International Red Cross Society.

    Your Son's effects have been gathered together and forwarded to The Royal Air Force Central Depository, where they will be held until better news is received, or in any event for a period of at least six months before being forwarded to you through The Administrator of Estates.

    May I now express the great sympathy which all of us feel with you in your great anxiety, and I should like also to assure you how greatly we all honour the heroic sacrifice you Son has made in the cause of humanity and in the service of The Empire.

Sincerely yours,

(Signed)

D.H.Burnside

(D.H.Burnside), Wing Commander
Officer Commanding,
No.427 Squadron, R.C.A.F.

8. The letter received by Tony Johnson's father telling him that his son was missing in action.

(Tony Johnson)

9. The main Luftwaffe interrogation and transit centre, Dulag-Luft, at Oberusal, Frankfurt-am-Main. The prison camp is in the foreground with the interrogation centre in the background, in front of the chimney stacks. *(Geoffrey Hall)*

10. German sentry on the gate at Dulag-Luft. *(Geoffrey Hall)*

11. Artist's impression of manacled prisoners being made to run 4 kilometres to Stalag-Luft IV in Pomerania in July 1944, whilst mercilessly being bayonetted and clubbed by their *Kriegsmarine* (Navy) escort. Drawing by former prisoner R.J. 'Curly' Franklin. *(R.J. Franklin.)*

12. The railway station at Gross Tychow where German atrocities took place in July 1944. *(Neville Ferneyhough)*

13. Stalag 11b at Fallingbostel in January 1945. *(via Tony Johnson)*

heating and cooking purposes, the ration was inadequate, and it was necessary to economize by the use of a 'blower' whenever possible.

The American food parcels contained a tin of powdered milk bearing the trade name of Klim. These tins were surely designed with *Kriegies* in mind to be used for the manufacture of air ducting and blowers. They were approximately five inches in diameter and, with the tops and bottoms removed, made a four inch section of air duct. From the solder salvaged from the hundreds of different cans, the sections were welded together to make ducts to channel fresh air to those *Kriegies* who, with intent to escape, were burrowing like mad six feet below the surface of the *Lager*.

Klim tins were also utilized to make blowers, table top gadgets for the speedy preparation of drinks and snacks – and 'glop'. By turning a handle a fan sucked in air which was then compressed and funnelled to direct a draught beneath kindling, such as coal dust, wood chips or cardboard. However, some operators in a particular hurry could crank the handle with such enthusiasm that the gadgets resembled erupting volcanoes – with fallout.

A bowl of glop was a firm favourite with all but a few *Kriegies*. A mixture of boiled barley and powdered milk it was extremely filling and not unpleasant to eat. When cold it had the properties of an all-purpose paste and was used to stick notices to the wall and pin-ups on bunks, and it was a sealant for draughts.

The goons barred the doors and windows well before darkness fell and opened up again after it became light in the mornings. There was a curfew in force while the barrack blocks were secured, and any *Kriegie* discovered in the *Lager* was liable to be shot on sight. The time spent in the rooms was generally occupied by reading books from the small library, studying, playing chess, bridge or any other card game. The gambling schools, which meant nearly all of us at one time or another, monopolized the table playing varieties of poker, pontoon and brag. With cigarettes being reasonably plentiful, in many instances the packets of cigarettes making up the ante were piled high on the table.

Those that wished to be alone would remain in their lower bunks, hidden from sight by cardboard screens made from Red

Cross cartons. They would emerge to brew up or make a snack, but were most unsociable. They were more to be pitied and, thankfully, there were not too many of them to a barrack block. They were weird.

There was a secondhand portable gramophone in the room. John Bulford would spend hours listening to long playing classical records while most of us were out in the *Lager* playing sport or pounding the circuit. It was the turn of the rest of the room to play an album or the Rogers and Hammerstein musical *Oklahoma*. The album comprised of five 45s, and by the time it could be played no more, we knew the score off by heart. When we exhausted the supply of gramophone needles, we resorted to using the teeth from combs. Amazingly they produced music, albeit so very soft. A packet of cigarettes or a bar of chocolate was sufficient in most cases to purchase a tin of needles from a goon, although needles were in short supply in Barth.

Before the morning *appell*, or roll call, there was a stampede to be one of the first to get to the latrine in the *Lager*. This early morning sprint was to try and wash and shave in tepid water before it was used up, and also to get a seat in one of the WC cubicles before the queues started to form. It was essential to take a paperback novel or a newspaper along as toilet tissues were non-existent. The cubicles had no doors, and there would be another row of *Kriegies* sitting opposite busily reading. Eventually, the pages that had been read would be torn out of the book and used as necessary. James Hadley Chase, a bestselling author of many raunchy novels, including *No Orchids For Miss Blandish* and *Road Floozie*, would have been less than pleased if he had known what they were being used for in the many camps throughout Germany. The *Volkischer Beobachter* and *Der Tag* newspapers, together with the Luftwaffe propaganda magazine *Der Adler*, were fit for little else than toilet paper.

Underneath the floorboards of the latrine there was a large sump to collect all the effluent, and from time to time it was emptied by a couple of Russian prisoners. Escorted by a goon, the Russians would bring a horse drawn sludge tank into the *Lager*. The contents of the sump would then be drawn off via a trap door at the end of the building, and then taken to be spread on the fields outside, and usually upwind of the camp.

Fifteen minutes before *appell* each morning, Percy Carruthers, the Hut Leader, would go through the barrack block to make sure we paraded in good time. Officially, only the sick could remain and be counted in their rooms.

To get on to the parade ground cum sports field, we had to pass through a gate in a barbed wire fence separating the *Lagers*. A goon had the job of unlocking the gate, waiting by it until the count had been completed, and then locking it again after the parade ground had cleared.

We formed into groups of a hundred *Kriegies* and in two columns in the centre of the parade ground. Goons were placed around the parade to try to prevent a miscount caused by *Kriegies* dodging from group to group to deliberately frustrate the goons conducting the count.

The Camp Commandant, *Oberst* Scherer, accompanied by *Hauptmann* von Miller, and other goons who made up his entourage, would enter the *Lager* and take up their positions at the end of the columns. Sergeant Barnes, the Camp Leader, who had been elected to replace Group Captain MacDonald, would call the parade to attention and salute the goon officers. We were then notified of any breaches of camp rules and the punishments meted out by the goons, usually seven or fourteen days in the cooler. The count would then get underway, conducted by two goons who had the intelligence to be able to count in multiples of five. One strutted along the front of the column wagging his forefinger between the lines of five *Kriegies* and counting out loud, while the other double-checked from behind.

If we were not in a really troublesome mood, parade lasted no longer than it took the goons to get their figures right. However, if it was decided to give them a bad day by having *Kriegies* hide in all sorts of places in the barracks or under the sandy soil, then we could be standing on the parade ground for hours before the 'missing' *Kriegies* were found. We had all the time in the world, even those who served time in the cooler for being bloody-minded.

As soon as the parade was dismissed there was a general rush to get through the gate in the fence and back to the rooms for another brew up or whatever. With a few hundred *Kriegies* converging on the gate and pressing to get through, the unfortunate goon who was waiting to lock up would be deliberately crushed against the barbed wire. On one occasion the bolt was carefully removed from his rifle while he was doing his best to avoid the stinging barbs. He would then have a final look round the parade ground to see if 'Butch' Reynolds was clear of the *Lager* before locking up. The dishevelled goon was just as likely to make his way back to the guardroom with a flower protruding from the spout of his rifle. We were past masters at providing our own amusement, however warped it might be.

'Butch' Reynolds had walked away from a Hudson light bomber that crashed into a dyke in Holland after being hit by flak. It was never discovered whether he was a born comedian, or whether he was completely round the bend as a result of the crash. He would come on parade last, either pretending to be a cowboy or a motorcyclist. Faithfully miming all the necessary actions, he would unsaddle and groom his horse beside his group in the column, and his prowess on his imaginary motor cycle put Steve McQueen's antics on a BMW in the shade. He would 'ride' around the parade at high speed, cutting up bemused goons, before parking his machine and waiting to be counted. One time he had us all, including the goons, in stitches while he went through the actions of mending a puncture. The goon on the gate was content to wait until the motor cycle was roadworthy again before he locked up. 'Butch' was a great character and the Freddie Starr of his day.

There was yet to be a successful escape from Stalag-Luft I, and all those who had surrendered bed slats had high hopes for the tunnel project that was progressing well and would soon be passing beneath the perimeter fence – although its planned course would take it dangerously close to the sump under the latrine.

Soon after the tunnel project began, it became apparent that the ferrets were more active in the camp. They crisscrossed our *Lager* prodding the sandy soil with long pronged sticks, obviously trying to detect a tunnel. They sent their dogs searching the space beneath the barrack blocks, and even went under themselves to investigate.

It was always a possibility that the Abwehr possessed some seismographic equipment to detect the sound of excavation as the tunnel neared the perimeter fence. If this was the case, then it would be sensible on the part of the Abwehr to let the tunnel be a form of occupational therapy for the *Kriegies* until they were about to break out. It would keep them from getting up to other mischief more difficult for the ferrets to discover.

The Escape Committee made it clear that the first out of the tunnel would be the selected few who had been instrumental in its completion, such as the diggers, the sand disposers, the lookouts and any others closely involved. After they had been given time to get safely away there would be a controlled exodus for those who wanted to take advantage of it. While the sand disposers and lookouts could be spotted from time to time, the diggers and other underground workers were kept out of sight until washed down and dressed.

There was a Polish pilot in one of the other barrack blocks who was an expert in copying the Luftwaffe and Wehrmacht metal insignia. After making the moulds from German soap, he cast the insignia from molten solder and silver paper. Blowers were used extensively in the process. Poles and Czechs excelled in this intricate and important work for escapers.

Circuiting the *Lager* was not only a popular form of exercise, it was a sure way of carrying on a conversation without being overheard by goons. It was also an effective method of dispersing sand from the tunnel. The sand was brought from the tunnel in pouches sewn into the trouser legs of those whose job it was to dispose of it. It was deposited on the ground by releasing slipknots in the trouser pockets. The *Kriegies* 'pounding the circuit' would further disperse the virgin sand which contrasted visibly with that on the surface of the *Lager*.

I suffered from claustrophobia and had used the Blackwall and Rotherhithe Tunnels with the greatest reluctance. Consequently, I made a point of keeping well away from the escape tunnel contractors in case I got roped in to do a stint underground. I was keen enough to get out of the camp, but unless absolutely unavoidable it would have to be some other way than by tunnel.

I managed to acquire some handmade wire cutters for a small fortune in cigarettes and tobacco but, whilst I felt that it was a useful tool for a potential escaper to possess, it was an effort to snip a prong off my dinner fork with it and I was not too convinced of my ability to penetrate the perimeter fences and coils of barbed wire before the goons turned their attention to me.

For days I would sit in the sand pretending to read or whittle pieces of wood to make a mouse trap. I waited for two things to happen; the cabbages on a *Kriegie*'s allotment to grow high enough for me to crawl unseen to the trip wire, and the goon in each of the towers overlooking the allotments to look away from my direction at the same time. I reckoned that once I had managed to cover the distance between the trip wire and the perimeter fence unseen, the fence itself would shield me from being spotted long enough for me to snip my way through.

I got as far as the trip wire on two nervous attempts, but with the limited cover the cabbages provided I felt so exposed and vulnerable I gave it up as a bad job. My flight to freedom scheme had to be abandoned completely when all the cabbages were harvested long before they were fully grown. The scheme was suicidal in any event.

All outgoing correspondence had to be written in pencil, and the monthly allocation of writing material was two lettercards and four postcards. It was normal for mail posted from the camp to arrive at its destination three months later. However, the time taken for incoming mail to reach the camp varied considerably. It took about three months to come from the UK, between five and six months from Australia or New Zealand and between seven and eight months from North America. All mail, outgoing or incoming, was subject to strict censorship, and one could only surmise what forbidden sentences the censor had blue-pencilled. Day after day I waited expectantly for my name to be called when the post arrived, but six months was to pass before that happy day arrived.

With few exceptions, after a week or so in captivity *Kriegies* suffered bouts of excruciating stomach pains. In my case the pains lasted for over a week, and I doubled up on my bunk believing I was going to die. The Medical Officer was little comfort. Although he was unable to provide medication, he did explain that my muscles were simply contracting – being nature's way of adjusting to the change in diet. After a week of agony and umpteen visits to the latrine, the pains began to subside and I then felt more sociable towards my room-mates.

It was great to once again appreciate the broad humour of the temporary male nurses from the north-east of England, Alan Hame, John Theckston and Larry Bone, whose folks all lived within a bus ride of Wigan Pier. Ken 'Marmaduke' Goodchild and Fred 'Andy' Anderson, like myself, had homes in the south of England. John Hooley, a veteran wireless operator from my squadron, was shot down a couple of months after I had been in the camp. He managed to get a bunk in our room and we became firm friends. A Canadian from Montreal, he brought news that 427 Squadron was now equipped with Halifax aircraft and operating from RAF Leeming. John and Bill were the only Canadians in the room at that time, but we were soon to be joined by American airmen of the 8th Air Force.

A batch of sprog *Kriegies* came into the camp each week, and they kept us up with the news from home. Most had been shot down during the preceding few weeks, but a number were from German hospitals and were recovering from terrible injuries inflicted in the air or by irate civilians. By midsummer 1943 the number of *Kriegies* in the camp exceeded the planned maximum capacity of 900.

The American 8th Air Force, equipped with Flying Fortresses and Liberator aircraft, was penetrating deeper and deeper into Germany in daylight. The many hours spent flying over enemy territory, coupled with the fact that the formations lacked essential fighter cover, resulted in the 'goddam lousy flak and the sonsofbitches in Fw 190s and Me 109s' causing a high casualty rate. Particularly during the Americans' raid on the ball bearing factories at Schweinfurt in August 1943, when sixty aircraft and 540 young Americans, were shot out of the sky by the Luftwaffe.
- The khaki uniforms worn by the Yanks, with gaberdine trousers held up by a snazzy chromium buckled belt, lightweight gaberdine

windcheater, fur lined trapper's hat and leather bootees, made a welcome change from air force blue.

Many new arrivals had suffered terrible burns to faces and hands, those parts of the body most exposed when wearing flying clothing. The unmistakable lines could be seen across their foreheads where helmets had afforded some protection from the flames. A few showed blistered skins, their burns considered unworthy of hospital treatment by the Germans. Those who had shrapnel wounds were unable to sit for weeks without some degree of discomfort – at least until their tender places healed. The more serious cases, those considered either mentally or physically incapable of ever again flying on active service, would eventually appear before a visiting Repatriation Board and be sent home on a prisoner exchange basis.

Collectively the Yanks were boisterous, brash, and pretty generally a pain in the neck. However, individually they could be the nicest and most generous people in the camp. Many lasting friendships blossomed between the Yanks and other Allied airmen in the camp and soon, with the swapping of items of clothing, it was difficult to tell the difference between nationalities.

Although I played most of the outdoor ball games, my preferences were volleyball, baseball and soccer. I was also very keen on running and boxing. During my training days in the RAF I was ranked a fairly useful welterweight, and things were fine so long as I was winning my bouts. If I failed to win, I lost interest in fighting and never considered making a career of the sport. It was something to do in the camp, and I spent many hours training with the other amateur boxers in the hut used as a gymnasium. Our trainer, Bob Waddy, was a Canadian and one of the hundreds of commandos captured on the Dieppe raid in August 1942. He had swapped identities with an airman and eventually turned up at Barth. It was difficult for me to understand why a soldier who could be presented with many opportunities to escape while on an outside working party, would change identities with someone else and finish up in a cage like Stalag-Luft I – yet it happened time after time. Bob was a boxing enthusiast and a formidable opponent in the ring.

A number of boxing contests were held in the camp theatre, and there were full houses on each occasion – the Camp Commandant and his senior staff monopolizing the ringside seats. The lack of fitness of the contestants determined that there should be three rounds, each of ninety seconds duration if the fighters managed to remain on their feet that long. Some bouts showed excellent boxing skills, while others bordered on slapstick comedy. A fighter would become physically exhausted, and be almost on his knees by the time the final bell was sounded. Those fans who collected their winnings after the contest, were only too pleased to carry their warrior back to his bunk where he would nurse his bruises and wonder why he ever bothered.

I had lost so much weight in the time I had been a *Kriegie* that, but for a couple of ounces, I would have weighed in at bantam-weight class. I looked like the guy who had sand kicked in his face before he enrolled for a body building course by Charles Atlas, but I had the footwork of a ballet dancer. I won my first fight by a technical knockout. My opponent had a habit of falling back on the ropes, to bounce off in a two-fisted attack. In the last round, more by luck than judgement, I caught him with a right to the jaw as he catapulted off the ropes. With a silly look on his face he reeled about the ring before slowly sinking to his knees. I was so amazed at what I had done, instead of delivering the *coup de grâce*, I helped the poor devil to his feet and walked him to his corner, apologizing profusely.

Despite the fact that I was a conqueror, Bob Waddy was far from pleased with my performance. I should have shown more of the killer instinct and finished the poor chap off instead of traipsing about the ring like a demented sugar plum fairy. My fans were more appreciative of my boxing prowess, and I walked unaided to my bunk prepared to challenge anyone – within reason.

Bill had somehow managed to acquire a secondhand guitar which he strummed for hours on end. And then he tried to sing along with his strumming, which did not please the other occupants of the room. He just wanted to sound like Gene Autry or Roy Rogers, the singing cowboys: instead, he sounded like a drunken fool in a pub singing contest. And when a few of us started to play our harmonicas it was bedlam, but it kept us from going round the bend.

Being a Welshman, Bert enjoyed playing rugby and singing in the choir. He had moved to another barrack block but we still exchanged social visits.

We had seen or heard nothing about about Geoff Hall since he was spotted at Dulag-Luft.

Chapter 8

V2 Rocket Testing at Peenemünde

A very talented drama society was formed in the camp and it provided popular entertainment by staging many of the successful West End plays. There were a few budding *Kriegie* actors even before the air force obtained their services, Donald Pleasance and Peter Butterworth being but two who improved their thespian skills by entertaining fellow *Kriegies*, and would play to a much wider audience in the postwar years.

The theatre stood alone in the *Lager* used for sport and parades. When a show was running, the final curtain was run down to enable *appell* to be completed and everybody was locked in the barrack blocks before dark. As with the boxing contests, the goons were always in attendance and occupied the front seats, tending to patronize the shows rather than to pop into Barth town during their leisure hours. Barth was reputed to have the highest incidence of venereal disease in the Third Reich, and *Kriegies* applauded the prostitutes and brothel keepers in our neighbouring town for their wonderful contribution to the war effort and trusted they would keep up the good work.

One morning following a show, *Hauptmann* von Miller addressed the parade to tell it that two foolish *Kriegies* had been caught trying to escape during the night. That they had not been shot in the attempt was an act of providence and as a punishment they would serve a long period of solitary confinement in the cooler. Even as von Miller was speaking, the two *Kriegies* concerned, 'Butch' Reynolds and his combine partner, 'Burglar'

Bill, could be seen in the *Vorlager* waving and yelling to us from their cell windows. We gave them a loud cheer as the goon officer was trying to make the point that anyone attempting to escape in the future took the risk of being shot on sight.

'Burglar' was yet another soldier who had at sometime or other changed identities, but was now trying to get out of a cage when he could have dodged away from an outside working party. He was from the East End of London, and insisted that he was a burglar by profession in civvie street and this was not his first time in prison. One had only to look at 'Burglar' to know he was telling the truth.

When they were released from the cooler, 'Butch' gave the following account of the incident. During the stage show the intrepid pair managed to conceal themselves in drums of lime in the theatre storeroom. The drums were large and were almost empty of the lime used as a disinfectant in the camp latrines. They waited until the theatre emptied and the parade had been counted and dismissed before they emerged from their hiding places. It got dark and the camp settled down. There was a logical explanation as to why the drums were not checked by the goons. They must have considered that no one but a madman would hide in a drum of caustic powder and they were probably right in this instance.

Plucking up their courage, 'Butch' and 'Burglar' left the comparative safety of the theatre and, crawling redskin style, made for the perimeter fence. Hugging the ground while prying searchlight beams swept the *Lager*, and waiting for the goon patrols to pass out of earshot, was an unnerving and slow business. 'Butch' was the first to negotiate the tripwire and reach the fence, leaving 'Burglar' who was in two minds whether to press on or scrub the whole caper and scuttle back to the safety of his lime drum, some yards behind.

'Butch' was about to start cutting his way through the tangle of barbed wire, when he became aware of a huge Alsatian inquisitively sniffing his ear, before sitting down comfortably to supervise the current bid to escape from Stalag-Luft I. He was quietly, but urgently, shush-shushing Rin Tin Tin away from the scene of operations, when the dog's handler walked up and pointed a Mauser L98 rifle at his head. 'Butch', realizing that the game was up, proceeded to entrance the goon with an Oscar winning performance on how to win friends and stay alive. It was doubtful whether he would have remained alive if he had been spotted by one of the goons in the *Posten* towers. He was standing in forbidden territory beyond the trip wire, the only excuse required by the goons to open up with their machine guns with murderous intent.

The pantomime at the fence had been observed by 'Burglar' who, having lost interest in what was now a farce, began back-tracking to the sanctuary of the theatre for all he was worth. He was soon discovered by the Abwehr goons.

However comical 'Butch's' account of the incident may seem, it was to their credit that they had thought up an ingenious plan to break out of one of the Luftwaffe's maximum security camps.

'Butch' eventually appeared before a visiting International Medical Commission, the Repatriation Board, pleading insanity, and was successful in being recommended for repatriation. The 'Repat' Board comprised of two Swiss and three German doctors, and their recommendations were final. Allied prisoners who were recommended for repatriation were usually swapped for an equal number of Axis prisoners at a neutral port, like Gothenburg in Sweden. *Oberst* Scherer was probably only too pleased to see the back of Sergeant Reynolds.

A cobbled road led past the perimeter fence to the north of the camp. Looking west, a short distance along this road was one of the Luftwaffe's largest flak training schools. Beyond this building could be seen the spire of Barth church.

The training courses at the school were attended in the main, by Luftwaffe personnel to learn the theory and practice of blasting Allied aircraft out of the sky. The occasional course for Italian *Regia Aeronautica* was fitted into the training programme. Whether the students were German or Italian, the sight of a prison camp almost filled to capacity with Allied air force POWs must have encouraged them to feel that their training produced results.

To the east of the prison camp and just visible a few hundred

99

yards along the road there was an airfield. It was rarely used for air traffic, but a battery of flak guns and two radar dishes could be seen close to one of the hangars. Except during the air raid on Peenemünde during the night of the 17–18 August, I never heard the 88mm flak guns open fire. However, one could be sure that the trainees would be taught to load the guns until they were proficient enough to dispatch shells at the rate of eighteen to twenty per minute.

Practical instruction for the trainees took place each weekday, the dummy target being an obsolescent Dornier Do 17 which droned back and forth incessantly all day long at a height of approximately 10,000 feet.

The Luftwaffe personnel would march smartly past the camp each morning lustily bellowing out their marching songs to return at lunchtime and at the end of the working day, still singing but with slightly less enthusiasm. We learned their songs by heart and competed with our hit songs proclaiming that Britannia rules the waves, and that we intended 'Hanging our Washing on the Siegfried Line' – if it was still there. The solemn rendering of 'Lili Marlene' was invariably a joint effort.

The Italians were a most undisciplined rabble, who delighted in provoking an interchange of barrack room language as they ambled past the camp. Their hosts deserved them, and all the Italians were short of were their hurdy-gurdies, monkeys and ice-cream carts. While the German trainees seemed to be able to track the Dornier with some precision, the Italians drove their instructors wild with their unbelievable antics with equipment on the airfield. The aircraft would be cruising in the west, while the guns and radar scanners would be pointing in every other direction, and this was no exaggeration. The instructors could be heard bawling impatiently at the trainees they were trying to teach to make war some of the time, rather than love all the time.

A *Lager* next to ours had just been completed in September when Italy capitulated, and the course of Italians at the flak school were marched straight into it. They were welcomed into captivity with a roar of delight.

One lovely summer's day we were startled by the ominous sound of machine-gun fire from one of the *Posten* boxes. In broad daylight and in full view of many of his room mates who were walking the circuit, a *Kriegie*, who must have gone completely round the bend, deliberately stepped over the trip wire and calmly walked to the fence and then, as though competing in an obstacle race, he began to scale the barbed wire. It was obvious to all that the man was sick and there was no intent to escape, and yet without any compunction, the goon in the *Posten* box snuffed out the life of the wretched soul. There was a near riot in the camp, but we respected the one-sided firepower of the goons.

The *Abwehroffizier* gave the usual talk on *appell*, reiterating his warnings about the foolishness of ignoring the trip wire notices. The death of the unfortunate prisoner should act as a deterrent to others. Like hell it did!

While pounding the circuit, *Kriegies* would often spot female labour working in the fields near the camp. When this occurred they would line the trip wire to get as close a look at the woman as possible, even though they were a few hundred yards away and appeared intent on what they were doing. The air would fill with cat-calls and wolf-whistles, accompanied by all manner of lewd suggestions on how they could better fill their time – in spite of the fact that closer inspection of the females revealed countenances not unlike Godzilla or the Wicked Witch. The condition of the goods would have made little difference to those *Kriegies* who had not been with a woman for years, if they could only have been let out.

Sprog *Kriegies* coming into the camp informed us of the repeated raids on the port of Hamburg by Bomber Command and the US 8th Air Force which took place over a continuous period of nine days. The operation, code name 'Gomorrah', created a terrible firestorm which roasted people alive and incinerated buildings. The casualties exceeded those caused by the Luftwaffe during the whole of its blitz on London in 1940–41. The raids cost Bomber Command eighty-seven aircraft, and another 400 of its aircrews perished.

Following the Hamburg raids which resulted in an appalling

101

loss of civilian lives, we became aware of a hardening of an already hostile attitude towards us by the German guards.

Infuriated by having his cities devastated by the Allied air forces, Adolf Hitler vowed that he would retaliate in due time by unleashing his secret V-weapons on London. Since the mid-1930s, Germany had been experimenting with a few 'unorthodox' weapons, including a jet-propelled flying bomb and a rocket. These *Vergeltungswaffen*, reprisal weapons, were being developed at an experimental establishment near Peenemünde, a small fishing village on the isle of Usedom in the Baltic. Usedom was one of a number of small islands in the estuary of the River Oder and was only fifty miles to the east of Barth. Hitler decreed that those heading the V-weapon projects, Wernher von Braun and Walter Dornberger, should spare no effort to perfect them and have them in full production by midsummer 1944.

The V-1 Flying Bombs, or Doodlebugs as they became known, and the V-2 Rocket Bombs, were intended to be launched from ramps sited in France and Holland within range of London. The V-1 was twenty-five feet long and had a sixteen feet wingspan, and it could carry a one ton warhead 150 miles at approximately 400 mph. The first one to be targeted on London was in June 1944, to be followed by 13,000 more before the launching sites were destroyed or overrun by the Allies. The V-2 was first successfully launched at Peenemünde in October 1942. It was forty-six feet long and also carried a one ton warhead. It could reach the speed of sound in thirty seconds, and climb to a height of between fifty and sixty miles before curving down to drop on an unsuspecting target about the area of London. Its speed on impact was estimated at 3,500 feet per second, and the first one zeroed in on Chiswick, West London, in September 1944. Five thousand more were aimed at London, Antwerp and Liege before the sites were destroyed or overrun. Unlike the V-1 Flying Bomb which could be heard jetting across the sky at a height of not more than a few thousand feet, the V-2, travelling at a speed much faster than sound, could not be heard coming, it was audible only when it exploded as it hit some real estate.

Lazing in the *Lager* on a warm summer day, we often noticed a distant white smoke trail climbing vertically in the sky to disappear into space. Although we assumed it was a rocket of some sort we did not realize that we were witnessing the final test flights of the V-2 before it was mass-produced and neither did we realize that these successful tests were heralding the dawn of space travel. In 1945 von Braun and his team surrendered to the Americans rather than the Russians, and they subsequently made an enormous contribution, not only towards the development of inter-continental ballistic missiles, but also to developing the necessary technology resulting in the American astronauts, Neil Armstrong and Edwin Aldrin, landing on the moon in 1969.

In October, six months after I had been taken prisoner, I was delighted to receive my first letters from my parents and Joyce. My parents waited for as long as three months before William Joyce, or Lord Haw Haw, announced my name with a list of other POWs during one of his propaganda broadcasts from Germany. Joyce had been corresponding with my parents and they let her know I was safe. It was a wonderful tonic to know that Joyce was still in love with me and that she was prepared to wait until I was eventually set free, and yet, I was very much aware that I was expecting a beautiful young woman to wait for an interminable period of time for someone in whose company she had spent less than twenty-four hours in total. There were also too many eligible young servicemen frequenting Darlington. It was a worry!

One afternoon the inmates of the camp were treated to a skilful flying display by the pilots of twelve yellow-nosed Messerschmitt Me 109 fighters belonging to the crack *Hermann Göring Geschwader* (Group). They circled the camp and airfield several times and then, after making some low passes followed by tight rolls, in line astern formation they landed at Barth airfield. After an overnight stay, they took off in the morning to engage the US 8th Air Force bomber stream of Fortresses and Liberators leaving their telltale contrails in the blue summer sky as they headed inland to their target.

Not long after this incident, Bomber Command sent a force of nearly 600 aircraft to destroy the V-weapon experimental establishment at Peenemünde. Most of us were asleep when the air raid sirens sounded in Barth and the flak school, followed by the camp lights being doused. Soon the sound of flak was accompanied by the drone of many aircraft passing overhead. Even the flak school opened up with its guns on the airfield and the noise was deafening. The tranquillity of Barth Bird Sanctuary was disturbed for about an hour while the raiding force clobbered Peenemünde. Peering from slits in the window shutters we managed to see some of the action, a few searchlights over Barth and bursts of flak high in the sky. We heard the howl of a stricken aircraft diving out of the bomber stream and then two parachutists were coned in the searchlights. Assuming they were our lads, we cheered.

On *appell* in the morning, the camp commandant praised us for being such sports and cheering the lucky escape by two of the crew of a Luftwaffe nightfighter that 'developed a fault'. We did not enlighten him.

The target at Peenemünde received extensive damage, and a number of civilian personnel were killed. A nearby garrison of soldiers was also hit resulting in heavy casualties. The raid cost Bomber Command thirty-eight aircraft, almost 200 aircrew would die, the rest would become POWs and we would get first-hand accounts of the action.

In view of the fact that the guns at the flak school were used in anger, albeit in a defensive role, during the Peenemünde raid, our Camp Leader, Sergeant Barnes, made a strong protest to the Red Cross representative when he next made a visit to the camp. Barnes argued that the camp should now be classified as being in a war zone and either it or the flak school should be moved forthwith. In accordance with the Geneva Convention prisoners should be afforded protection from the warring parties. The Abwehr, and much less the German High Command took scant notice of the Red Cross or the ramblings of an RAF sergeant, despite the fact that he represented over a thousand *Kriegies*, and no relocation took place. We were quite content to stay where we were.

As other members of my squadron were shot down and turned up at the camp, I was kept fairly well up to date with the news. The heart-throb film star, Clark Gable, took time off from being a rear-gunner in the US 8th Air Force to visit the squadron and present it with the MGM logo pins at the official 'adoption' ceremony. The pins were not worn on operations, however; not that the Germans were anxious to own MGM badges, but rather the pins identified the squadron.

When the squadron transferred from Croft to Leeming, Croft became the base for two Halifax squadrons namely 431 (Iroquois) and 434 (Bluenose) Squadrons. The inhabitants of Croft and Dalton-on-Tees had to endure a lot more noise with the increased activity on the airfield, but there was an upturn in annual profits at the Croft Spa Hotel and the Chequers public house – and at Mary Pearson's sandwich takeaway.

Those of us who were the last to fly Wellington aircraft in Bomber Command, would have been privileged to have operated in Halifaxes or Lancasters. They had a much longer range, were faster and could carry twice the bombload of a Wellington but were just as vulnerable at the receiving end of a flak or cannon shell.

Work on the tunnel progressed slowly through the summer months and many of us had only five bed boards left to support us in slumber. There were many accidents caused by flying bedboards and tempers flared. Many of us felt that in view of the discomfort we had to endure because of the tunnel project, we qualified for a place at the end of the queue when the breakout eventually took place. It was of no concern to a number of *Kriegies* who were reluctant to leave the 'sanctuary' of a prison camp and would 'sweat it out' until the end of the war. It was a question of personal choice. If given the opportunity I would have plucked up enough courage to crawl through a dank, sandy-walled tunnel to freedom. However, it was not to be.

One day the tunnel lookouts were puzzled to see a small mechanically propelled road roller trundle into the *Vorlager* and pull up outside the Abwehr office. A short time afterwards, it was started up again and driven into our *Lager* and then began to circle the barrack blocks. Its presence then became clear, and the tunnellers were evacuated just before the roof caved in. The roller had found a weak spot and the ground had subsided beneath the weight of the roller. My heart went out to the tunnellers who had

105

spent months underground – it was back to the drawing board, although nobody managed to escape by a tunnel during my stay at Stalag-Luft I.

It was announced on *appell* that we were leaving Barth in a few days' time and heading for East Prussia to Stalag-Luft VI at Heydekrug. Stalag-Luft I was to hold American air force officers after our departure. Our quality of life was going to deteriorate drastically as the months went by. The 'good' life was over.

The fact that the tunnel project had 'fallen through' was only a temporary setback for a *Kriegie* named George Grimson. George was shot down in a Wellington aircraft of 37 Squadron, based at RAF Feltwell, during the night of 14-15 July 1940 while targeting Hamburg. His was the only aircraft to be lost by Bomber Command that night and he was one of two survivors of the crew of five, although ninety-seven aircraft were dispatched to bomb industrial targets and lay mines. He was an escape artist of extraordinary talent, daring and determination, whose aim was to cause the Germans as much inconvenience as possible. He soon became fluent in the German language and it is said that his first escape was achieved simply by giving his German escort's behind an almighty kick and making a run for it. Soon to be recaptured. George learned to avoid this vexation of the spirit for longer periods outside the wire. A natural loner, both inside and outside the wire, he still managed to escape with another *Kriegie* from Stalag-Luft III before it became an officers only camp and all NCOs moved to Stalag-Luft I, Barth. George remained at large for some weeks before being recaptured and once more spent time in the cooler. It was at Barth that I got to know this most exceptional character, although only by sight because he was not in the compound for long.

The day before we moved out of Stalag-Luft I at Barth, George stepped over the tripwire dressed as a goon maintenance worker and carrying a homemade ladder. In fluent German he passed the time of day with the goon in the *Posten* tower and was about to check for an electrical fault in the floodlighting circuit. George then calmly propped the ladder against the fence and climbed it. He then bridged the gap between the two fences with the ladder, which he rested against the outer fence. After going through the motions of fixing a lamp and trying not to electrocute himself in the process, he descended the ladder to stand outside the camp. Then shouldering the ladder and waving cheerio to the goon, he sauntered off to freedom. It was an audacious escape that infuriated *Abwehroffizier Hauptmann* von Miller, and considerably lessened the promotion prospects of the goon in the *Posten* tower when details came to light upon George's subsequent recapture some weeks later.

Chapter 9

STAMMLAGER-LUFT VI, HEYDEKRUG, KÖNIGSBERG

We left Stalag-Luft I in October 1943 and retraced our steps along the cobbled road to Barth railway station. In preparation for the long journey to East Prussia, we had adapted spare shirts in which to carry our worldly possessions. The tails of the shirts were sewn together, and then the cuffs were also sewn to the tails to make shoulder straps. Everything was stuffed into the homemade rucksacks via the collar opening. It was surprising how much the rucksacks held and how weighty they became.

At the railway station we were each given a loaf of bread and a lump of sausage to last us until we reached Stalag-Luft VI. We were then shepherded into cattle trucks and packed so tightly there was just enough room to sit with the rucksack. It was my first experience of travelling like an animal and I was not too impressed. When the sliding doors were closed, the only interior lighting was provided by four small windows, two on each side of the truck near the arched roof. These windows were criss-crossed with barbed wire on the outside. The doors were secured on the outside by the goons.

Once the train got underway, we took it in turns to stand at the windows and give a running commentary when anything of interest was taking place and to see what the goons were up to when the train stopped.

During the time at Barth, *Kriegies* managed to acquire all

manner of sharp instruments, and we were soon beavering away at the timber floorboards above one of the truck's axles. One *Kriegie* had even managed to acquire a bayonet which he put to good use, whittling away at timber that was still tough to chip despite its age.

Our first long stop was at Stettin (now Szczecin), a Baltic port at the mouth of the River Oder, where we were shunted onto a siding for a few hours. We were allowed out of the trucks in batches and taken under escort to a public toilet on one of the platforms. Apart from any other consideration, this privilege gave us a good opportunity to stretch our cramped limbs and to take in the layout of the marshalling yard. By this time a number of the trucks had been vandalized, and when one hole was sufficiently large enough to allow a small person to squeeze through, he would be off as soon as it was safe to drop out of the truck. Before this could happen at Stettin, however, we were on our way again.

On the journey between Stettin and Danzig (now Gdansk), there were many more stops in sidings. Trains passed us heading west, packed with wounded soldiers, giving us some indication of the ferocity of the fighting along the River Dnieper. It was a terrible war!

On the way it became necessary for the train to make a number of unscheduled stops at rural stations. The tin buckets placed in the trucks for toilet purposes were quite inadequate and frequently needed emptying. The doors would be slid open, and the goons would stand well back while we piled onto the track to hastily drop our trousers and foul the permanent way. A few hundred bare bottomed *Kriegies* squatting along the up track was truly a sight to behold. The goons standing guard every few yards lost all enthusiasm for their work, and would turn away as though to dissociate themselves with the unsavoury business. They were confident that a *Kriegie* was not likely to make a dash for it with his trousers round his ankles.

One time some civvies and services personnel waiting on a station platform were treated to the rare spectacle of several hundred *Kriegies* squatting and performing well along the track.

The engine driver shunted the train forward the length of a few trucks, and exposed the exhibitionists to those waiting on the platform. The females shrieked and turned their backs in disgust, while the menfolk remonstrated with the goons for allowing such a disgusting display. This episode was one of embarrassment to all concerned, but it provided many a laugh during the rest of the journey to East Prussia.

Travelling for hour upon hour through the Polish Corridor, along with thirty-nine other sweating bodies in a cattle truck, is not to be recommended under any circumstances. Bearing in mind that many *Kriegies* were suffering with diarrhoea, the sticky combination of smells, both human and farm animal, in such a confined space was something to which we soon had to become accustomed. Cigarettes helped to some extent, although the smog they generated caused chronic coughing spasms. Also the draughts caused by the fast moving train made our eyes stream. It was a most uncomfortable journey by train.

Watching from one of the windows, I would be surprised at the primitive agricultural implements still being used by those working on the land; some workers were pulling ploughs and actually performing the work of shire horses. There was very little mechanization to be seen on the farmlands and in the villages. Groups of people waiting at level crossings were either on foot or were in possession of a pedal cycle. Occupied Poland was an unhappy country, and it showed on the faces of its inhabitants.

The hole in the floor would soon be big enough to squeeze through. My wire cutters came in useful, but I was more convinced than ever that they would not have cut through a strand of barbed wire. We all 'chipped' in by taking turns at gnawing away at the timber, until the palms of our hands blistered and bled. It was a race against time, as every mile we travelled was taking us further away from the friendly occupied countries of the west. Sweden was an option, but it would be difficult to smuggle aboard a ship bound for that country. The ports were watched and the Baltic Sea was patrolled by *Kriegsmarine* (German Navy). There was also the possibility that one of the many sympathetic Polish families could be contacted and provide shelter until an escape route was organized.

The progress of rail rolling stock, non-essential to the German war effort, was so frustratingly slow. It took no less than forty-eight hours to travel the distance of just over 200 miles between Barth and Danzig. On arriving at Danzig, we were shunted into a siding in the huge marshalling yard. Although it was almost midnight when we settled down, the yard was well floodlit and goons with their dogs patrolled along either side of the train. However, as the night wore on, the goons' patrols became less frequent and their presence less obvious. Excitement mounted as we waited patiently for the right moment for one of us to try his luck.

Suddenly the stillness of the night was shattered by the sound of someone shouting in German, and at the same instant several shots sounded near to our truck. This commotion was followed by a lot of goon activity, culminating in a khaki-clad figure being carried away by two stretcher-bearers. After a ten minute lull, there was another flurry of activity as the entire guard detail of goons was summoned on duty to surround the train. The doors of the trucks were then slid open and a goon climbed into each one, where he was to remain to watch over us for the rest of the journey. Our resident goon soon found the hole in the floor, and smilingly wagged a forefinger reprovingly. We had been naughty boys.

At the next halt we learned that it was an American who had been shot, possibly fatally, while trying to escape. He had covered no more than a few yards before he had been spotted by a goon and shot. Although we were saddened by the turn of events, it was, however, a fact that sudden and violent death was now a way of life. I had mixed feelings about the tragedy. On the one hand I could not help feeling quite vindictive towards the Yank who had frustrated any further chance of escape, and on the other hand, it could be said that he was the one to test the temperature outside – and found it bloody hot.

After a change of locomotives at Königsberg (now Kaliningrad), we eventually arrived at Heydekrug. The camp was five miles from the border with Lithuania and twenty-five miles from the Baltic Coast, the nearest town being Tilsit (now Sovetsk). It opened in June 1943, and was larger than Stalag-Luft I at Barth.

It was quartered with four *Lagers* 'A', 'K', 'E' and a spare, with the *Vorlager* butting on to *Lagers* 'A' and 'K'. The camp had been built on flat, sandy terrain, in the middle of a large forest clearing. Initially it was built to contain British, Commonwealth and American airmen of NCO rank. Each *Lager* was equipped to accommodate 2,000 *Kriegies*, and those who had been transferred from Dulag-Luft and Stalag-Luft III in June occupied 'A' *Lager* which was full to capacity.

After passing through the Abwehr for the strip search and documentation, we were given the 'freedom' of 'K' *Lager*. As at our previous camp, everything was new in the *Lager* and we could choose our rooms and bunks. We were given a talk by the British Man of Confidence who, in this camp was Warrant Officer J. A. G. 'Dixie' Deans. He was a sergeant pilot flying a Whitley aircraft during a raid on Berlin in September 1940, when he was shot down and taken prisoner after baling out over the German–Dutch border. With his long experience as a *Kriegie* he soon established himself as a neutral leader who quickly earned the respect, not only of his 'flock', but also of the Germans with whom he came into contact. Apart from looking after the welfare of the *Kriegies* who had elected him to office, he did everything possible to assist a viable escape plan. He was the one who carried the secret radio, codenamed 'Canary' from Stalag-Luft III to Heydekrug right under the inquisitive noses of the Abwehr, who would have been delighted to put their hands on it. Contained in the motor compartment of a portable gramophone, this valuable piece of 'homemade' equipment was known to only a few trusted *Kriegies*. Shorthand notes were made of BBC broadcasts, a transcript of which was brought round to each barrack block and quietly read out to an intent audience. This way we kept abreast of events outside the barbed-wire.

The barrack blocks were similar to those we left at Barth, and also featured a gap beneath the floor allowing inspection from the outside of the buildings. Each block contained nine rooms, each large enough to accommodate fifty *Kriegies*. Once again we had the full complement of bedboards. The table had bench type seating and there was a black cast iron stove with a month's supply of coal bricks. A corridor ran the length of one side of the building, with a latrine seating two at the end.

The barbed-wire fences, tripwire and *Posten* towers, were standard as at Barth, but there were many more warning notices stuck in the ground just behind the tripwire. A typical example was: 'DANGER OF LIFE! WE SHOOT! WE SHOOT WITHOUT WARNING OR CALL WHENEVER YOU TOUCH OR SURPASS WIRE OR POLE'.

Each of the three *Lagers* that were occupied was a self-contained unit with its own leader. Sergeant Victor 'Nobby' Clarke, who succeeded Sergeant Barnes at Stalag-Luft I, was the leader in 'K' *Lager*. As 'E' *Lager* began to fill with American airmen, Technical Sergeant Frank Paules was elected their leader. Dixie Deans in 'A' *Lager*, by virtue of his experience and seniority, spoke for the whole camp and had unrestricted access to the camp commandant.

The three *Lager* leaders and the padre were the only *Kriegies* permitted free range within the confines of the camp. They met from time to time to discuss welfare matters, exchange information and convey the many grievances to the camp Commandant through Dixie Deans.

The two Abwehr officers were Major Reshel and *Hauptmann* Thome and, in a camp that was to eventually hold over 8,000 in a period of a few months, there was quite a considerable establishment of ferrets.

The daily *appell* was conducted in each *Lager*, where the parade ground also doubled as a sports field. Games where a ball is used had to be played with some restraint to avoid the loss of balls in the rough beyond the perimeter fences. Any ball that came to rest in the prohibited zone behind the trip wire could only be retrieved at the discretion of the goons in the towers. In most cases they were menacing and uncooperative, returning the balls to the parade ground overnight. As the balls were in short supply, this meant that a game had to be abandoned in some instances. Where a game was an important one and there were many cigarettes at stake, some of us took on the might of the Luftwaffe just to retrieve a football or a baseball. We would stand in groups near to where the ball lay beyond the tripwire, and as soon as we were satisfied that the goons in the *Posten* towers were looking elsewhere, one of us would dash for the ball and get back in the crowd before being seen, or in some cases, before the goon could aim a gun. This was a silly and dangerous game, but with nothing better to do it was a means of getting one over on the goons – and a ball back into play.

All RAF aircrew NCOs automatically received promotion on the anniversary of the date they qualified as aircrew. In the case of Dixie Deans, he was a sergeant at the time he was shot down but he had been in captivity long enough to qualify for promotion to the rank of warrant officer. Sergeants shot down before May 1943 would be promoted to warrant officers by the time they were liberated. Notification of promotions would be received several weeks after being promulgated in the UK – the *Lager* leader would hand a chit to the person concerned, shake his hand and congratulate him. There would not be a booze-up to celebrate the rise in rank and pay. There would be a quick calculation to decide how much the rise in pay was worth and, to ensure that the money accrued interest during captivity, a two-thirds allotment would be made over to next-of-kin to bank. This arrangement was not always satisfactory, however. Because of hardship at home, genuine or otherwise, some single men returned only to find their nest egg had been spent as soon as the allowance had been drawn from the post office. The lump sum they received from the RAF averaged out at £1.6s.0d (£1.33p) for every week in captivity.

As soon as I got settled in the barrack block, I decided that it was an opportune time to pull out of the combine I had joined at Barth. The combine was too big, and there were endless arguments concerning the unequal portions of food doled out and the unsuitability of the menu to some. Nobody volunteered to be 'mother' to hungry *Kriegies* for long, particularly after being threatened with violence. I went into a combine with John Hooley because there were less to satisfy but even so one had to be very careful to avoid a quarrel over rations.

The attitude of the goons towards us was getting even nastier and we had not been in the camp long before there was a shooting. A *Kriegie* named Kenwell had finished a bit of washing and, perhaps absent mindedly, he tossed the bowl of dirty water over the trip wire. This must have incensed a goon in the tower nearest the place where Kenwell had been doing his laundry, for he raised his rifle, took aim, and shot the unsuspecting dhobi-wallah in the arm. Sergeant Kenwell did not hang around for another shot, he dashed for the safety of his barrack block. He had to have treatment for a shattered bone and, after the wound had been dressed, he spent fourteen days in solitary confinement in the cooler for good measure. We took great care from that day on when disposing of dirty water.

Bert Symons and Bill Ostaficiuk were still in the same *Lager*, but now in a different barrack block to mine. The fact that they were living apart from me was not because of any strained relationship. It was simply the way things turned out and, in the long term, I would be glad that we had separated. About this time, however, we did learn on the grapevine that Geoff Hall was in 'A' *Lager*. He came into our *Lager* with a group of theatre-goers to see a show, and made contact with Bert before returning to his *Lager*. Geoff was the last before Steve to bale out of our aircraft and managed to evade capture for something like forty-eight hours. He had been experiencing hallucinations before he was captured near the village of Nennig, south-west of Trier. He was captured by an army corporal accompanied by an aggressive member of the Hitler Youth Movement. The youth was the more antisocial of the captors and, prodding Geoff with a bayonet, kept insisting that the *Engländer Terrorflieger* should be summarily executed. Although Geoff was hungry and rather lightheaded and prepared to let events take their course, he strongly resisted any suggestion that he should be sacrificed at the instigation of an adolescent in uniform but still wearing short trousers. Geoff was spared and taken to Trier and then to Dulag-Luft. After a period of interrogation, he was moved to the main *Lager* until Stalag-Luft VI at Heydekrug was completed. He was in one of the first batches of *Kriegies* to occupy 'A' *Lager* in the new camp in June 1943.

In one delivery of mail a *Kriegie* received a most distressing letter from one of his relatives. The fact that the writer of the letter inferred that the *Kriegie* was a coward for surrendering to the

115

enemy, could not have been more clear if a white feather had accompanied it. These insensitive missives, perhaps written in ignorance rather than spite, were by no means uncommon. The 'Dear John' letters were other morale destroyers which, in many cases, were the first and only correspondence *Kriegies* received from their girlfriends or fiancées.

These painful, and sometimes bizarre, letters were displayed on a notice board for all to see and either have a jolly good giggle or jerk a few tears in sympathy. Examples of the type of letter that were displayed or otherwise circulated the camps were as follows:

A *Kriegie* in his second year of captivity was to learn that he was the father of a bouncing baby boy, and what should it be called? We all had a name for the newborn.

The wife of another poor lad rejoiced in the fact that she was pregnant by a Yank called Chuck, but 'not to worry because he was a decent guy who was going to send some cigarettes regularly'.

'Cousin Fred has been taken prisoner in Sicily, and mum was wondering whether you could pop round and see him.'

'Do you manage to get to any dances?'

'It's now four years since you were shot down. Mother and I have discussed it and have decided that it would be better if I divorced you.'

'I'm calling our friendship off, as I would rather marry a 1944 hero than a 1939 coward.' The recipient of this callous piece of news from home was a pilot who was seriously wounded when he was shot down during the early months of the war. We considered this a classic.

Once every three months kinfolk could send 'personal' parcels to *Kriegies* if they so desired. Their maximum weight could not exceed 10lbs and they contained clothing and shoes. Every parcel received at the camp was examined by the goons, and many items of clothing and shoes would be damaged beyond repair in the search for secret messages or contraband. A *Kriegie* requesting a pair of slippers would have to wait a total of six months for a reply – post took about three months each way. One hopeful asked for a nice warm sweater in a letter to his girlfriend. Six months later she wanted to know if she should knit a vee or roll neck, and what colour he had in mind. I am sure she meant well, but I am not sure he ever received the sweater. In many cases insensitive post was one of the causes of mental illnesses which tended to accelerate the physical deterioration of many *Kriegies*, thus sapping the willpower and stamina necessary to endure the marathon marches across Poland and Germany that were to be our lot in a few months time.

A frequent vexation of the spirit occurred when the goons aroused us during the early hours of the morning, to make us stand in our underwear, or pyjamas should one be so lucky, while our rooms were systematically searched. They would search for escape items and the secret radio receiver which we referred to as the 'Canary'. One of the Abwehr sergeants, a sadistic Ukranian bully, towered above us. His own subordinates were terrified of him, because he would show them no mercy. I nicknamed him 'Attila'. While a ferret would be bent over a bunk diligently searching for any hiding place, the inviting posterior would be too much of a temptation to 'Attila'; he would give the goon's backside a hefty kick and then curl up laughing. He was a dangerous psychopath whose aim in life was to inflict injury to others and hope for some retaliation so that he could have reason to draw his Luger and kill. One day I was to be his victim – just for kicks!

It was a beautiful summer's day, and I was leaning on the wooden rail surrounding the static tank that was being used as a model boating pool. I was suddenly aware of 'Attila''s presence beside me, and at the same time of an excrutiating pain in my right foot. He had penetrated my foot with his pointed probing stick, challenging me to do something to ease the pain. I did. I knocked away his stick and half ran, half limped, away as fast as I could and got lost in the barrack blocks. I still bear the scar and, as I dared not seek medical attention, it turned septic and took several weeks to heal. I avoided 'Attila' from then on.

The American 'E' *Lager* soon filled to overflowing and subsequent intakes came into our *Lager*. I had to share my bunk with an air-gunner named Pedro Fernandez. He was an interesting character from San Antonio, Texas. He insisted that it was one of his ancestors who killed Davy Crockett at the Alamo chapel. He would hold the room spellbound with his yarns of prospecting for gold in the Yukon, of keeping a whorehouse in Whitehorse, and being a film extra in westerns. He had a never ending repertoire of bawdy rhymes and ballads, including the classics 'Eskimo Nell' and 'Dangerous Dan McGrew'. I could recite them off by heart, but they are not the sort of entertainment for a meeting in the church hall.

When the freezing weather came the Canadians were able to indulge in their national game of ice hockey. Buckets of water from the static tank and latrine were relayed along a human chain and sloshed onto a section of the parade ground. After the first layer froze, the pitch was marked out with a blue powdered dye. Then more water was thrown onto the area until it was fit to skate on. The ice hockey equipment was provided through the YMCA by charitable organizations in North America, the skates being the strap on type rather than the skating boots. I was surprised to find how much the hockey sticks helped balance, and I was soon playing a reasonable game although I was by no means an expert. It was something different to take an interest in.

Although for some weeks we had been receiving less than a full parcel of food each, it was necessary to prepare for, in my case, the first Christmas in captivity. This meant putting some food by so that we could have the nearest thing to a slap-up meal on Christmas Day. Biscuits were saved to powder down and mix with raisins to make a cake. Prunes were for dessert. For booze we fermented raisins and swede jam to make a concoction that was guaranteed to paralyse, blind or produce acute alcoholic poisoning, if consumption exceeded half a cupful. We were treated to a one-off delivery of American food parcels specially packed with Christmas in mind, for they contained a tin of turkey breasts and also a tin of Christmas pudding. On Christmas Day we were visited by a couple of the more acceptable goons who would do favours to our mutual advantage. They joined in the spirit of Christmas and staggered back to the *Vorlager* hoping they were not in for a surprise posting to the Russian Front. The day's festivities were rounded off with a sing-song, the only musical instruments being combs and mouth organs – and Bill and his guitar. He was unable to get the hang of that thing somehow.

A lot of our time in winter was spent outdoors pounding the circuit. This was a method of economizing on the coal ration, to use it for cooking and some warmth overnight. The two blankets and a greatcoat were quite inadequate in an East Prussian winter, when the wind never ceased to howl.

One pastime for the *Kriegies* promenading round the circuit, was to throw snowballs at the goons in the *Posten* towers. This was great fun until the object of our attention turned nasty and menacingly aimed a machine gun in the direction of a rapidly dispersing crowd of *Kriegies*. With so many snowballs zeroing into the *Posten* tower with unerring accuracy, it was little wonder that the goons would turn nasty. That was the object of the exercise.

On a social visit to Bert Symons on one occasion, I found him composing poetry. He was not alone in this form of pastime, as many *Kriegies* fancied themselves as budding bards. Bill struggled with his guitar, and spoke more like Noel Coward every day.

Over in 'A' *Lager*, Geoff Hall studiously passed his time by wading through the books he obtained from the *Lager* library. He hoped to enter the teaching profession some day, and was studying the subjects, particularly English grammar, which he felt would be of benefit to him at a teachers' training college. During the winter months I endeavoured to advance my education to some degree, as it had suffered during my schooldays by having to attend six different schools and leaving at the age of thirteen years to go to work to supplement the family budget. I also studied the German language, just in case I had to make a practical use of it some day. There were plenty of goons on which I could try out the exercises. And, although they would listen to what I had to say with interest, their expressions soon turned to bewilderment as they walked away slowly shaking their heads. Nevertheless, as the months passed my German improved. I also read a dog-eared copy of the German National Socialist Party's blockbuster by Adolf Hitler, *Mein Kampf*. Gripping stuff!

I was to be concerned at a letter I received from Joyce, which was taken up by a lengthy apology for sending me a letter breaking off our relationship. Fortunately, this letter of reconciliation overtook the 'Dear John' letter in the mail, otherwise I would have really been in the doldrums. By then we had been parted for nearly a year, and I prayed so much that our love would endure until I got home.

Chapter 10

Happy Twenty-First Birthday

Word filtered through the grapevine that George Grimson had been recaptured and was in 'A' *Lager* having served his time in the cooler. After his cheeky escape with a ladder from Stalag-Luft I at Barth, he had spent weeks in Poland moving from port to port along the Baltic coast trying to set up an escape route with the help of the Polish Resistance. He was playing an extremely dangerous game, but nevertheless he made some useful contacts before he was recaptured.

Soon George was on the run from Stalag-Luft VI. Again in uniform, he simply tagged on to the end of a squad of goons leaving 'A' *Lager*. Once he had got into the *Vorlager*, he nipped into one of the buildings and quickly got rid of his uniform, revealing civilian clothes. He then calmly strolled out of the main gate of the camp and was away again.

Just as the Germans had rounded up all Allied officers known to be habitual escapers and concentrated them in the maximum security of Colditz Castle, similarly all air force NCOs who were seasoned escapers were brought together in Barrack Block 12 in 'A' *Lager* of Stalag-Luft VI. Besides George, there were escapers named Flockhart, Leaman, Lascelles and at least a dozen others who had been *Kriegies* for many years. Most spoke German as well as the natives, and they were dedicated to escaping to freedom and causing the goons as much unpleasantness as possible.

Since the camp opened, the escape organization in 'A' *Lager* had endeavoured to establish some kind of escape route from a Baltic

121

port, preferably Memel in Lithuania, or from Danzig, both of which were frequented by Swedish merchant ships. Escapees like George Grimson, and two other hut mates named Callender and Lewis, had been making some progress in this direction until their luck ran out. As all contact with them was lost, it could only be assumed that they had been recaptured and summarily shot.

It was about this time of the year, towards the end of April, that the goons clamped down on these irregular departures from the camp, following Warrant Officer Leaman's thwarted escape bid. Dressed as a goon, Leaman managed to get past the guard on the gate between 'A' *Lager* and the *Vorlager*. However, as he was crossing the *Vorlager*, he was directed to go into the guardroom. He was instantly recognized and thrown into the cooler. From then on anyone leaving the camp by the main gate had to produce some means of identification.

During the long months of captivity certain *Kriegies* in 'A' *Lager*, and particularly the occupants of Barrack Block 12, had managed to cultivate one or two goons, said to be Ukrainians, who had become disenchanted with the way the war was progressing and wanted a good word put in for them when the day of reckoning came. These collaborators were of great assistance to people like Grimson when their guard duties were on *Lager* gates, particularly the main gate. They were also indispensable in many other ways, such as providing articles of uniform, local maps and railway timetables, etc. Once caught up in the web of intrigue, if necessary they would be blackmailed into fully cooperating; if the Abwehr were informed of their treachery it would mean a firing squad. Goons were known to commit suicide when pressure got too great for them – such were the stakes.

Compared to 'A' *Lager*, the escape organizations in our *Lager* and the American 'E' *Lager* were quite amateurish affairs. When it came to trying to get goons to perform favours for us, we were not in the same league. It was for this reason many of us in 'K' *Lager* were quite envious of Dixie Deans and his closed shop.

On Saturday, 12 February, 1944, I can remember the day so well, we stood in the wind and cold for morning *appell*. While waiting for the Commandant and his staff to appear from the

Vorlager, we had our morning snowball fight. Each side was a thousand *Kriegies* strong. With the best aimers in the front ranks, and the logistics crews maintaining stockpiles of snowballs at the back, soon there were nothing less than flying avalanches arching through the air. Around two thousand snowballs airborne at any one time was a lot of snow moving about, and it was inevitable that a goon would become a target. One minute he was enjoying watching the snowballing, the next he looked like a snowman himself – with the barrel of a rifle protruding from the top.

There was always a ceasefire during the count. The parade was called to attention by Vic Clarke and I was then surprised to hear *Oberst* Hörbach shout out my christian and surnames as I was called forward. I was at a loss to know what was in store for me as I trudged over to stand before the Commandant. Vic Clarke's face gave no clue. *Oberst* Hörbach's face broke into a benign smile as he brought a silver key from behind his back. He handed the key to me, shook my hand, and then wished me a very happy twenty-first birthday. The goons grinned, Vic grinned – and I grinned with sheer relief as I realized that it was indeed my birthday. With a feeling of embarrassment, I saluted, about turned, and rejoined my squad – to a chorus of 'Happy Birthday to You'. This chorus was slowly taken up by the occupants of the other *Lagers* who, apart from Dixie, would not know who all the fuss was about. With over 5,000 *Kriegies* wishing me a happy birthday in a snowbound POW camp in East Prussia, I felt very humble – but it made my day!

It was a one off presentation which, so far as can be ascertained, was something that had not previously happened in the camp, nor happened again for anyone's birthday before the time we were evacuated in July 1944. The key was about two feet long, and made from a piece of wood. It was then covered with silver paper. My room mates and crew had got together to make the key and, with the help of Vic Clarke and Dixie Deans, managed to talk the Camp Commandant into making the unusual presentation. I treasured the thought and the key, and I have never received a more surprising birthday present.

With the Wehrmacht on the retreat from the Red Army in the

Ukraine, they brought with them many Russian prisoners who were being put in the spare *Lager*. The prisoners were skin and bone, having trudged through all weathers with so little food that they were starving. We learned that many had died as a result of starvation and the atrocious treatment by the Germans on the terrible journey to the camp. They did not receive Red Cross parcels and the little that we could spare, we threw into their *Lager* at the risk of being shot. In turn, the Russians would scramble for the scraps of food at an even greater risk of being shot by the merciless goons. It was so pitiful to see how the Russians were being treated and yet be unable to do very much to alleviate their suffering.

The consignments of Red Cross parcels reached the camp less regularly due to the disruption of the German transport system by the Allied air forces and, as a result, we were having to tighten our belts even more to eke out the rations. Not only were the parcels having to be shared amongst two or more persons per week, but the German food issue was also at a minimum. We had all passed a stringent medical examination before being accepted for aircrew duties, and enjoyed strong constitutions which undoubtedly helped us to cope extraordinarily well with the increasingly difficult conditions at Stalag-Luft VI. Surprisingly few *Kriegies* were seriously ill. They dared not be – the sick bay would be unable to manage.

We would often see Luftwaffe aircraft fly over the camp towards the east to support their troops locked in combat with the Russians. Occasionally a crippled fighter aircraft would return from the arena, its pilot probably wounded and just managing to keep the aircraft in the air. The sight of one of these shot up aircraft would result in a loud cheer.

With the approach of the warm weather, I spent hours in the gym skipping, and generally having a good workout within my limitations, to build up sufficient stamina to survive three rounds. Bob was still as enthusiastic as ever for his team to gain supremacy over the teams in the other two *Lagers*, in particular the 'E' *Lager* team of Americans with its loud mouthed trainer. Bob would have us exercising and sparring until we were ready to drop, usually offering himself as a human punchbag in the ring. On one occasion he took such a hefty punch on the side of his head that it burst an eardrum. We kidded him that from that moment on he always appeared just a little punch drunk.

After one highly entertaining and successful boxing contest, the loud mouthed American boasted that he had a fighter that could lick anyone in the camp. He threw out a challenge that Bob could not refuse to accept. Bob felt that he had just the right man to beat anyone the Yanks put in the ring: an ex-public schoolboy who was an orthodox boxer with a rapier-like straight left and a devastating right cross which was necessary for him to use only once or twice to put his opponent on the canvas, out for the count. His style would have made the 8th Marquis of Queensberry ecstatic.

During the weeks before the contest we tried to find out what kind of opposition we were up against, but the Americans were not prepared to give anything away except that he was to be billed as the 'Bearded Marvel' and was a welterweight.

The night of the 'big fight' was soon upon us. I boxed in one of the supporting bouts and, although I won, it was by no means an easy win and I was glad to hear the bell in the final round. I was unable to repeat the performance at Barth when I was able to produce a knockout punch – however technical.

When the 'Bearded Marvel' climbed into the ring he looked like a trained gorilla. Short, thickset, with beady eyes glowering from a head of black hair. His demeanour in his corner while waiting for the bell suggested that, rather than being an amateur, he was in the professional class. There was no way that this could be proved, and I thanked my lucky stars that I was a flyweight and no contest for this animal. He could have been eating T-bone steaks at an airbase in Cambridgeshire no more than a couple of months before the 'big fight'.

In the event, the fight turned out to be an excellent contest between a shrewd orthodox boxer and a streetfighter. For two ninety-second rounds there was little to choose between them except their different styles. We felt that at any moment our boy was going to produce a right to finish the fight, but the Yank's

125

beard must have softened the blow. In the third round the Yank's stamina and punching power won him the fight on a technical knockout after an onslaught of haymakers. Bob Waddy was inconsolable. So far as he was concerned, the Americans would boast about beating the goddamned Limey for weeks to come.

Another tunnel was being excavated in the *Lager*. The same architects and contractors were in charge of the project. This time the entrance would be in the latrine, with the tunnel running under the boundary fence to surface in the open near some trees. The site had been selected near the fence where a little road roller could not get although, being in the latrine the air was foul right to the working surface of the tunnel.

Many *Kriegies* thought up schemes to escape which they wanted to put into practice. However, even if a scheme was approved by the camp Escape Committee, which comprised Dixie Deans and a number of 'elders' in 'A' *Lager*, they would have to wait for the OK to put the plan into action. Staff Sergeant Walker in 'E' *Lager*, and a pal, were presumably given the OK to try their scheme out. They joined the morning sick parade to the sick bay in the *Vorlager*, where they concealed themselves in one of the buildings to wait for darkness to fall. Steps were taken to cover for their absence on the evening *appell*. Around 02.15 hours they left their place of concealment and, making good use of the buildings for cover, they stealthfully made their way to the fence which they intended cutting their way through. They had nearly reached the fence, when they were suddenly bathed in the glaring beam of a spotlight shining from one of the *Posten* towers. There was nowhere for them to run and hide. Instead of being cut down by a burst of machine-gun fire as they stood with their hands raised in surrender, an Abwehr sergeant came out of the shadows, held a Luger to Walker's stomach and pulled the trigger. The American died almost instantly.

It remains a mystery why, after a period in the cooler, the other American was allowed to return to 'E' *Lager* to tell the tale. From the information we received in 'K' *Lager*, the incident had all the hallmarks of a set up, meaning the goons had prior warning of the escape plan and had been waiting in ambush. There was always more than one enemy to beware of in a prisoner of war camp.

Of course, through Dixie Deans, Frank Paules made a formal complaint to the Camp Commandant, and the crime was also reported to a visiting ICRC representative. It was also stressed that the Germans had tried to cover the murder up by not giving Walker a formal burial. Life went on.

Half a dozen *Kriegies* managed to climb out of the tunnel and make for the trees before the goons closed in and greatly disappointed a group still waiting in the latrine for the signal to crawl to freedom. They were all suitably dressed to mingle unobtrusively with the local populace outside the wire. It was a terrible disappointment to all concerned in the project. I had even less faith in tunnels, although for many they were the only hope of freedom.

The warm summer weather began to bring out those *Kriegies* who had been in semi-hibernation during the winter months. And with the increasing numbers pounding the circuit, there was also an eye-catching selection of spring fashions on show, particularly in leisurewear. A pipe-smoking, bearded, Yank skinhead, sporting the latest Johnny Weissmuller style briefs and flying bootees, did not look out of place on the circuit. Uniform trousers in shades of blue and khaki, cut and shaped to make chic shorts together with a whole range of silly hats, some being just brims cut out of cardboard and pulled over bald heads, while others were fashioned from cardboard boxes to keep the sun from those who turned red and burnt easily.

I was one of those skinheads who had my head shaved to discourage fleas and lice, and to see if my hair would eventually grow more curly. German lice seemed to prefer head hair rather than facial hair, but most of their bloodsucking energies were concentrated about the waist, the ankles and the crotch. The spiteful little blighters would use their hypodermic lances twenty-four hours a day, but were more active at night when their hosts and providers were trying to sleep. Heydekrug lice were the most voracious of parasites and survived my every effort to exterminate them.

One morning in May, while assembling for *appell*, we were puzzled to find that the guard had been doubled as though the

127

goons anticipated trouble. When the Camp Commandant and his usual entourage appeared on the parade ground, his greeting with Vic Clarke seemed more formal than at other times. The parade was called to attention, and there followed a brief pause while the Commandant, head bowed, nervously shuffled some papers. With some embarrassment, he then informed the parade that there had been a mass escape from a tunnel at Stalag-Luft III, despite many warnings of the consequences. Our outburst of cheering was short-lived as he continued with the terrible news that forty-seven (later amended to fifty) Allied officers had been recaptured but, regrettably, were killed 'while again trying to escape'.

It took little imagination to realize that there had been a mass execution. The probability that every shot fired at forty-seven escaping officers proved fatal was very remote indeed. The men had been murdered in cold blood. Feelings were running dangerously high in the camp, and only the firmness of Dixie Deans prevented what could have been a very nasty situation. Commonsense prevailed.

Instead, the camp embarked upon a campaign of goon baiting, and frustrating the counts on *appells*. We tried to keep the goons busy all day by having *Kriegies* hide themselves so that they were overlooked when the sick in the huts were counted, or by squad jumping to make it appear that there were more in the camp than there should be. All good fun and it annoyed the goons tremendously. On one occasion they had to resort to a sheep count by herding us all to one end of the *Lager*, and then get us to walk to the other end in batches of five. Only when the *Kriegies* who had hidden themselves were eventually found and marched off to the cooler, were the goons able to satisfy themselves that the head count was correct.

Signwriters in the *Vorlager* got busy and new notices appeared against the tripwire and on the notice boards to the effect that escaping was no longer a sport, and the Führer had given strict orders that in future any prisoner found trying to escape, or at large, would be shot on sight and without warning.

Once again Dixie lodged a formal complaint, and once again it was completely ignored by the Germans.

On the slightly brighter side: a good day for me was when I received a fifth instead of a sixth or seventh of a loaf of bread, or Johnny Hooley and I managed a grand slam at bridge at a fag a point. In the mail from home our folks forecast that 'it' would not be long now, or 'it' would soon be all over. We had to keep our chins and peckers up and, what with all the fighting going on, we were in the best place until 'it' was over.

During the summer months there was an extended curfew from 22.00 to 06.00 hours, and the goons were generally punctual in barring and unbarring the doors and windows. For some unknown reason, or unless he was anticipating the events to follow, a goon unbarred the door of a barrack block in 'K' *Lager* at 05.50 hours one morning. An American, Staff Sergeant Nies, thought he would take advantage of an early morning wash before the rush. Wearing only shorts and carrying a towel, he left the barrack block only a few minutes before the end of the curfew at 06.00 hours, and strolled casually across the *Lager* towards the latrine. Whilst Nies had not paid too much attention to the time, a goon in one of the *Posten* towers had. He raised his rife, took careful aim, and shot the unsuspecting *Kriegie* in the stomach. As the fatally wounded man lay on the ground, his life ebbing away, the goons threatened to shoot anyone leaving the barrack blocks to go to his aid. He died as he was being carried to the sick bay on a stretcher.

Reg Goodenough, a *Kriegie* I was to escape with ten months later, was so moved by this latest atrocity, that he composed the following poignant poem:

THE EARLY MORNING WASH

> The early morning chorus
> Of birds seemed strangely hushed,
> As that silent lonely figure
> Lies crumpled in the dust.
>
> The towel across his naked chest
> Will dry a different hue,

But he will not be caring
His washing days are through.

But who will tell his mother
That he died today because,
He left his hut too early
For his daily morning wash?

In the murder of Sergeant Nies, the Germans had once again demonstrated their complete disregard for human life and the evil bastard who pulled the trigger would feel safe in the knowledge that he was obeying orders.

The 'Canary' chirped out the wonderful news that the Allies had gained a foothold in Normandy, acting, of course on the master plan by the *Kriegie* strategists. We were not concerned whether the Supreme Commander was Eisenhower, Montgomery or Shirley Temple, just so long as we were home for Christmas. With the Russians advancing from the east, and now a Second Front, Hitler and his army were now between a rock and a hard place, and we hoped the German High Command would convince their Führer that it was futile to fight on. It was another forlorn hope but, at least, the end was now in sight.

As soon as we were dismissed, we returned to the barrack blocks and celebrated with the hidden stocks of illicit brew.

The goons were visibly shaken by the news of the invasion and, with prohibition still in force, they were at a loss to understand the antics of some of the drunken *Kriegies*. Goons boasted that their Panzers would soon push our armies back into the sea, just as they had done at Dunkirk and Dieppe. Of course we laughed in their faces, but we could not dismiss the possibility out of hand. We were satisfied that the Allied air forces had air supremacy, and this would dictate how soon the ground forces would be able to break out of the beach-heads to take the offensive to the heart of Germany. And the barrack block war strategists would plan every move. We dare not contemplate another Dunkirk.

The months of June and July were sunny and warm, but despite the hot weather the goons had neglected to empty the latrine sump.

It was beginning to hum. The latrine sump was normally emptied by two Russian prisoners under the supervision of a goon. They would come into the *Lager* with a horse drawn four-wheeled cart, on which was bolted a large cylindrical tank with a round glass observation window at the rear end. The tank was fitted with two valves, a one-way unit at the top, and a simple two-way gate valve at the bottom rear. A number of spectators would gather around the cart to watch the goon carry out the procedure necessary to draw off a tankful of foul effluent. And while the goon was engrossed in preparing the Heath Robinson sludge gulper, the hub nuts on the cart would be loosened so that a wheel, perhaps two wheels, would come off on the way to the spreading fields. We were sabotage specialists.

A Russian would connect one end of a hose to the bottom valve, and drop the other end through a trapdoor into the sump. Opening the top valve, the goon would squirt in some petrol and follow it with a lighted match. The gases from the internal explosion would exit through the top valve which, in turn, would seal the tank to create a vacuum. The other Russian would then open the bottom valve and the best part of a tankful of effluent would be drawn from the sump. It would take several trips to drain a latrine sump.

It was a lovely day and some *Kriegies* were sunning themselves, some pounding the circuit, and others playing or watching football. Suddenly there was a violent explosion which shook the camp – the latrine had blown up. The force of the explosion had flattened the walls and the roof had caved in. Those of us in the open were showered by some of the contents of the latrine sump arcing indiscriminately through the air. It was disgusting. Barrack blocks were instantly camouflaged. The referee blew his whistle, believing that for the time being at any rate, the football match should be abandoned.

Over the weeks of warm weather the latrine had filled to capacity, and a build up of methane gas had made the structure into a latent bomb just waiting to be detonated. All *Kriegies* were prone to flatulence to some degree, and were attuned to the sounds ranging from thunderclaps to barely audible wheezes, but this was something altogether different. Those of us who had been

131

christened with the contents of the sump were not very pleased and less so those sitting hunched in the cubicles, either in deep meditation or reading their paperbacks, when some careless wally lit a cigarette and dropped a lighted match into the sump to ignite the gases. The building had collapsed like a deck of cards, and there were a number of casualties with later unconfirmed reports that two of the victims had died from their injuries.

I was at the wrong side of the football field when the explosion occurred, and the blast, with its accompanying waste matter almost blew me off my feet. Some moments passed before any of us could fully comprehend what had happened and, as we ran to the latrine, I was amazed to see a stark naked man, completely unrecognizable because he was covered from head to foot in sewage, emerge from the wreckage and stagger about blindly. The first priority was to rescue anyone trapped in what was left of the latrine, and this perhaps explained why the bewildered man was initially bypassed by those first on the scene. His hut mates arrived and commiserated with him, but from a distance.

After we had satisfied ourselves that nobody was still trapped in the latrine and the traumatized and otherwise poorly were allowed to the sick bay, those of us who had only been be splattered rinsed down in the static water tank.

Three Russian POWs were allocated the unsavoury task of clearing and rebuilding the latrine. As it took a few days to restore the much needed building, it provided the opportunity to pass them a few hundred cigarettes and what little food we had to spare.

In July 1944 we were notified that we were to prepare to evacuate the camp at short notice. With the Red Army offensive gathering momentum and rolling back the Wehrmacht, and Vilna in neighbouring Lithuania falling to the Russians, the German presence at Stalag-Luft VI had become untenable, especially as there was still a *Lager* crammed with Russian POWs who were treated terribly by their guards and were no more than skeletons in what clothing they had. We were to move as soon as transport became available.

The American airmen in 'E' *Lager* were the first to leave the camp and, as they marched out they were treated like conquering heroes by those still in the camp.

The day after the Americans left, I was one of a batch of 800 British and Commonwealth airmen from 'K' *Lager* to move out. Like the Americans we would finish up at Stalag-Luft IV at Gross Tychow in Pomerania. The inmates of 'A' *Lager*, along with those left in 'K' *Lager* headed for Stalag 357, a huge mostly army POW camp at Thorn in Poland. Gross Tychow was eighty miles south-west, and Thorn ninety miles due south of the port of Danzig.

As we ambled out of the camp en route to Heydekrug railway station shouldering our DIY rucksacks, Johnny Hooley carried our food supply, while I looked after the clothing and other essentials such as they were. It was a parting of the ways so far as the rest of my crew, Geoff, Bill and Albert were concerned as they were in the contingent bound for Thorn, it being just a question of which hut you were living in when the goons split 'K' *Lager*. These *Kriegies* set light to their barrack blocks before passing out through the gates. It annoyed the goons but not to the extent that any punishment was meted out – they were not inclined to want to hang about any longer than necessary.

Although we were not aware of it at the time, our real suffering at the hands of the airmen and sailors of the Reich was about to begin, and many of my fellow *Kriegies*, some close friends, would be executed or die as a result of maltreatment at the hands of our captors. Some during the last days of the war would lose their lives, becoming the casualties of 'friendly fire' from the RAF 2nd Tactical Air Force.

From this time on there would occur many incidents that would stress many of the men touched by them, and there would be obvious signs that whatever syndrome they suffered they would have to live with them for the rest of their lives – without compensation.

Chapter 11

CRUISING IN THE HELL SHIP *INSTERBERG*

The inhabitants of Heydekrug had turned out to line the roadside to watch the raggle-taggle procession of *Kriegies* pass on its way to the railway station. Children standing with their mothers probably tasted chocolate for the first time in their lives, generously handed to them by prisoners elated by the absence of barbed wire. Old men scrambled to collect liberal sized cigarette butts tossed away by the more 'wealthy' prisoners. Many of us, not knowing what the future held or where the next meal was coming from, wisely hung on to everything we possessed. We wondered how long it would be before these people were watching Russian tanks and troops passing through Heydekrug, to disturb the peaceful isolation from the sounds and ravages of total war.

One *Kriegie* wore a cardboard placard across his chest proclaiming 'Uncle Joe for King', which was soon confiscated by a goon. Uncle Joe Stalin had a large following in the camp, simply because his army was on the offensive and advancing towards East Prussia while Allied troops were still bogged down in their Normandy beach-heads. As soon as they broke out and went on the offensive, and to liberate Paris, the Eisenhower and Montgomery team would top the popularity polls in the Stalags.

As soon as we arrived at the railway station we were loaded into cattle trucks that were waiting in a siding for us. The trucks had been adapted for the transportation of human beings and in them we experienced what must have been the feelings of millions of poor souls who, having been considered unacceptable to the

Master Race, were conveyed to concentration camps and their deaths in the gas chambers. It was a feeling of utter degradation. The trucks were divided into three sections, and were partitioned by two barbed wire screens across the width of the truck. The two end sections held the prisoners, and the centre section was for the guards. We each had sufficient room to sit with our knees up under our chins, while the goons had room to lie on the floor. As the goons were also being posted to the new camp there were one or two in each truck.

It was rumoured that we were going to Memel, and there embark on a ship that would sail to Germany through the Baltic Sea. None of us were too enthusiastic about sailing through the submarine and mine infested waters, including the Germans.

Two miles out of Heydekrug, we passed through Tilsit (now Sovetsk) and then a few hours journey to Memel. At Memel, the train went on to the quay and came to a standstill opposite a rusty old coaster, bearing the name *Insterberg* on its stern. The ship had a U-shaped hull, comprising two holds, one fore and the other aft of the bridge and, sandwiched between the bridge and the engine room, were the stores and crew's quarters. The holds were covered, except for a small hatch to give access.

Like the animals embarking on the Ark, we trooped across the gangplank two by two, one *Kriegie* to be steered to the forward hatch and the other to the aft hatch. We were made to leave all bulky baggage on the deck, but I managed to hold on to my rucksack with a little food in it. Descending a twenty-feet steel ladder to the bowels of the ship, I found myself standing on the propeller shaft housing, and it was necessary to make use of footrests to finally stand in the well of the hold. In the half light the hold looked cavernous and a potential deathtrap. The floor was coated with a thick layer of coal dust, and there were pools of stagnant water in the well. The arched top of the propeller shaft housing was occupied by *Kriegies* along its length, and they were going to regret their choice of place to sit down. To find a place to settle, I had to clamber over bodies until I was perched on the side of the hull. It was a most uncomfortable position, but I had no option other than to get used to it. If I lost my balance, I would roll on to

135

Kriegies below me, and although they would have cushioned me from injury, there would be many moans and groans of protest. The hold was soon filled with 400 *Kriegies*, each with just sufficient room in which to squat. There were sanitary arrangements, but it meant picking one's way through knee deep humanity, climbing an energy-sapping ladder to the deck, and then going through an embarrassing procedure of relieving oneself on a wooden chute overhanging the side of the ship. The guard at the hatch was armed to the teeth. In addition to a sub-machine gun, several stick grenades were stuck into his belt.

The crew of the ship appeared to be Russian, and they were controlled by a detachment of *Kriegsmarine* – German Navy. The *Insterberg* was escorted by an E-Boat, which continually circled the ship during its voyage.

The hatch was battened down overnight and, in the pitch darkness of the hold, we were left to worry over all sorts of nasty things that could befall us during the voyage, such as striking a mine or being torpedoed. There was only about a quarter of an inch of steel plating between me and the Baltic Sea. I tried to form some sort of contingency plan to put into practice should there be an emergency – anything to increase my chances of survival. Everything was so nightmarish. The darkness of the hold had a claustrophobic effect on me, and I was most unhappy with the whole situation.

Many *Kriegies* suffered from seasickness and, although the ship had not yet put to sea, there was soon an overpowering stench of body odour, diarrhoea and vomit. There was no ventilation and the air was also thick with tobacco smoke. It was too much to expect men to refrain from smoking – it was the only nerve steadying remedy available to us.

The ship did not put to sea until the following morning. Suddenly the engines came to life, causing the ship to vibrate excessively. This was accompanied by the sounds on the quayside as the crew went through the casting off procedure. Then a loud clanging noise came from the propeller shaft with every revolution of the propeller, and this was to continue for as long as we were at sea. It must have been sheer purgatory for those who chose to sit on the shaft casing.

During the seventy-two hours we were on the *Insterberg* the Germans provided us with neither food nor water. To climb the ladder and be allowed on deck to gulp in fresh air were the moments of pleasure on the voyage. On one visit, I thought I could make out the coastline of Sweden in the far distance off the starboard beam. However, I quickly dismissed any thought of diving overboard and trying to swim to the neutral country. I would not get very far from the ship before I was riddled with bullets from a sub-machine gun and, in my physical condition, I would soon succumb to the waves anyway.

From time to time the hatch would be opened and a goon would peer into the gloom of the hold to see if we were behaving ourselves. One great fear was that one of his grenades would drop out of his belt and fall amongst us. Whilst it was not supposed to explode with its pin still in, that was no consolation – it would still give someone a nasty bump on the head. There must be some ICRC rules that forbade the transport of POWs in a coal boat through the Baltic.

Many of the 800 prisoners sweltering in the holds became seasick and, in the absence of medication, all those unaffected could only sympathize and endure the stench.

It was by far the longest voyage I had been on. Once my parents treated me to a day trip on the *Royal Daffodil* paddle steamer from London Tower Bridge, navigating the River Thames to Southend Pier. Ice-cream, candyfloss and cockles, and then back again – they were happy days!

We had to be very careful with what little rations we had with us, such as biscuits and cheese. This was all John Hooley and I had to eat during the time we were on the ship. Jake Akehurst, who was in our party, managed to get hold of a can of water from right under the noses of the goons, but there was only sufficient to wet our lips. The heat in the hold was oppressive in the daytime and not a lot cooler at night. The sound of snoring was made even louder by the acoustics of the hold.

In comparison with many in the same predicament, health wise I had fared exceptionally well, apart from the painful stomach cramp as a sprog *Kriegie*, and my brief encounter with 'Attila'.

137

However, I was concerned about the weight I had involuntarily lost while on the *Insterberg*; weight that I could ill afford to lose. At night we would try singing songs like *It's a long way to Tipperary* to keep our spirits up, and also to show our captors that we were far from downhearted in spite of the atrocious conditions. I was still worried about how I would manage to get out of the hold in an emergency, and I came to the conclusion that there was no way I could get to the hatch before *Kriegies* were clinging to the steps like wasps swarming around a stick of rock. I was most concerned about my safety.

On 19 July, after three long days at sea, we berthed at Swinemünde, about thirty miles east of the V-weapon research establishment at Peenemünde. Being unaware that we were near land, as the ship scraped along the quay, my first thoughts were that the noise was caused by the horns of a mine. I was relieved to hear the sounds of the crew mooring the vessel and lowering the gangplank.

It took some exertion to climb the ladder, but as we walked ashore in bright sunshine, it was a wonderful feeling to take in fresh air and to feel concrete under my feet. It was a warm sunny day and we had docked in a large bustling naval base. Opposite the train of cattle trucks, and astern of the *Insterberg*, the battle cruiser *Lützow* was riding at anchor with its swastika pennant fluttering in the breeze. Offshore a flotilla of U-boats basked beam to beam in the sunlight.

As we assembled to be counted and allocated a cattle truck there was an air of uneasiness. The *Kriegsmarine* heavily outnumbered our normal guards; they were much younger looking, and could have been fresh from the Hitler Youth Movement – fanatical and dangerous teenagers. They glowered at us and, holding their rifles across their chests with fixed bayonets, they seemed to be spoiling for a fight. Our goons had acquired a few more dogs.

We became more troubled when the *Kriegsmarine* produced a large supply of manacles, and began to chain *Kriegies* together by the wrists in pairs, two feet of chain linking the two bracelets. These extreme measures by the combined services of the *Kriegsmarine* and Luftwaffe gave us some concern for our future.

John Hooley and I were not going to be manacled if we could help it and by holding hands, and joining those manacled without being seen, we were still holdings hands when the supply of manacles ran out – leaving no more than half a dozen of us free. We were then crammed into the cattle trucks.

Standing behind the barbed wire partition, our black grimy faces streaked with sweat, we resembled paid up members of the NUM in the pit cage after a stint of working at the coalface – we also stank like a camel market. No sooner had we settled in the trucks, when the air raid sirens sounded about the base. Our arrival at Swinemünde had coincided with a daylight air raid, and within minutes the smoke making machines sited about the complex were belching out a choking smokescreen which blanketed everything, rendering the vessels and harbour installations difficult to see, and accurately bomb, from the air. To be manacled, caged and a target for Allied bombers did cause us some concern. Things were getting out of hand.

As the suffocating smoke found its way into the trucks, and the goons put on their gas masks and helmets, we could only cough and retch until tears streamed down our dirty cheeks. Soon the steady drone of the bomber force could be heard, to be accompanied by the sound of heavy flak. As the aircraft flew overhead, the nearby *Lützow* and other warships opened up with their big guns, the noise rising to a crescendo until it seemed that all hell had broken loose. The truck nearly jumped its tracks as bombs rained down, some exploding too near for our peace of mind. At the height of the raid, the flak, coupled with the earth trembling explosions, produced a terrifying cacophony of sound. Our guards had every reason to panic and seek shelter under the trucks. Some were trying to hide alongside railway sleepers and they trembled uncontrollably with fear.

We felt the train was in a vulnerable position as it stood in the open on the quayside and the danger that a bomb would toss our truck into the sea was uppermost in our minds. We would have no chance to escape as we sank to our watery graves.

After forty minutes of savage conflict, the sound of battle abated, to be replaced by the noise of urgent activity around the base. The goons rejoined the trucks, and it was very apparent that they were displeased with having to endure something so warlike as an air raid; it was infinitely more dangerous than guard duty in a *Posten* box, where the odd *Kriegie* could be murdered from time to time without punishment. They would soon be getting their own back on the *Terrorflieger Gefangenen* in their charge.

A pall of smoke still shrouded the base when the all clear was sounded, and this prevented an assessment of the damage caused in the raid and, possibly, it saved our train from being lined up in the bombsight of some Allied airman. The *Lützow* and our cruise ship *Insterberg* appeared to have survived the attack unscathed.

After waiting another hour or so in the sweltering heat of the truck, we left Swinemünde for the seventy-five miles journey to Gross Tychow, near Schneidemühl (now Pila) in East Pomerania, arriving in the early afternoon. After alighting from the train, all 800 prisoners were paraded beside a platform. We were surprised to see that the *Kriegsmarine* were still with us, some of whom were wearing light running shoes. About one in three was armed with a sub-machine gun.

We were called to attention as a Luftwaffe officer, later to be identified as *Hauptmann* Richard Pickhardt, one of the Abwehr officers at Stalag-Luft IV, mounted a trolley to address us. For ten minutes he stormed and raved about the destruction of German cities by *Luftgangsters* and *Terrorfliegers*, mentioning Berlin, Cologne, and his home town, Hamburg, and stressed the civilian death toll. His tirade was intended to agitate and inflame the passions of the *Kriegsmarine*, and there is no doubt that he succeeded. The situation was getting more frightening by the minute, and there was nothing at that stage to confirm that there was a prison camp at Gross Tychow. At Pickhardt's signal, we were made to jog from the railway station and through the village. The local civilians spat, jeered, and waved their fists at us, and were obviously trying to encourage the goons to make life even more unbearable for us.

As we left the built up area and turned onto a cart track cutting a sward through tall pines, the escort turned on the pressure. Out of the sight of the civilians, they instantly set about us with the bayonets, rifle butts and dogs. From a steady trot, we were made to stampede with the dogs snapping at our heels, and were running, weaving and dodging to avoid the jabbing bayonets and swinging rifle butts. The *Kriegsmarine* were in their element showing no mercy. They enjoyed every moment of it. With knives they would cut away packs from *Kriegies*' backs, knowing they could well contain cigarettes and chocolate. Anyone falling by the wayside through exhaustion, would be bayonetted or struck by a rifle butt. I found myself dodging and leaping over fallen comrades who had either stumbled or dropped with exhaustion, with the partners in chains desperately trying to pull them to their feet while under attack themselves.

As I passed one goon standing astride a fallen *Kriegie*, I heard a pistol shot. Believing that the goons were intending to shoot the stragglers, I found enough energy to accelerate until I was up with the front runners. Things would have been easier if I had got rid of my pack, but I did not want to face John Hooley, whom I had lost in the panic, if he came through still carrying the food in his rucksack. He would not have been too pleased to find he had no change of clothing.

It was a terrible experience because, for all we knew, we were going to be herded into a clearing and massacred. The Germans were quite capable of doing that.

After about two miles the stampede began to lose its impetus. So many *Kriegies* had either collapsed through exhaustion or were lying seriously injured on the trail. The head of the column had thinned out, many of the older goons leaving the *Kriegsmarine* to keep up with those still running like hell.

I was determined to make a dash for it into the woods if the opportunity presented itself, but realized that this was exactly what Pickhardt wanted. Every few hundred yards there was a manned machine gun almost hidden by the trees and foliage.

In one part of the lane, many of us had the pleasure of trying to trample a fallen goon into the ground. He must have been at death's door after being jumped on by heavy booted prisoners. One went completely berserk, repeatedly smashing his guitar over the head of an Alsatian dog until he killed it. It was absolute panic and chaos.

After two-and-a-half miles and what seemed an eternity, we ran into a clearing with a POW camp in the middle of it. John Hooley and myself, not being hampered by manacles, were in front as the column concertinaed up to the front gate. We collapsed with exhaustion, but I was delighted to be at the gates of a prison camp. To me it was a kind of sanctuary.

After regaining our breath, many of us wanted to go back down the trail to assist our fallen comrades but were prevented from doing so by the *Kriegsmarine*. It took an hour or so before the last of the stragglers, including the walking wounded, joined us at the gates of the camp. While we waited, we held an inquest touching upon the unsociable behaviour of the goons, especially the *Kriegsmarine*. We soon came to the conclusion that the whole episode had been orchestrated by *Hauptman* Pickhardt in a calculated attempt to force us to break ranks so that the machine gunners could mow us down 'whilst attempting to escape'.

After releasing all those who had been manacled, the *Kriegsmarine* left to take their loot of cigarettes, chocolate and other items of prisoners' property back with them to Swinemünde, and probably to boast about their day of action with the enemy.

Chapter 12

STAMMLAGER-LUFT IV, POMERANIA

When we were eventually allowed into the camp, we were told that there was no permanent accommodation yet available for us. The camp was still in the course of construction, and not enough barrack blocks had been completed to accept an intake of 2,600 prisoners over a period of forty-eight hours. Our contingent, along with a number of Americans, had to share a large marquee with just enough room for each to bed down on the ground. This was to be our shelter for a few uncomfortable weeks, without running water or proper sanitation. Water had to be pumped from an underground spring. In view of the traumatic events during transit from Heydekrug, we were content to rest for a few days to recuperate.

John Hooley and I had been lucky. Not only had we survived the ordeal unscathed, but we had also managed to hang on to our rucksacks containing a change of clothing and a little food.

It was a common sight to see a *Kriegie* with a bloodstained slit, or slits, in the seat of his trousers; or with other injuries about his head and face. He would be one of the walking wounded who, although in need of stitches, bandaging, splints or antiseptic, would have to go without any sort of medical attention – there were no such facilities in the camp at that time. With the wounded unable to sit comfortably they spent hours in the prone position waiting for the injuries to heal although, due to a lack of resistance to septicaemia, this took weeks or months, sometimes only after repatriation. Good-humouredly, we would rag our friends about being too slow in dodging the objectionable treatment being meted out by the goons or, in the case of the Americans, purposely taking punishment to qualify for the Purple Heart. One comedian boasted that when he was jabbed by a bayonet, he accelerated so fast that he ran off the blade before the goon had time to withdraw it. It was a typical example of British humour in adversity; humour the Germans could never understand or appreciate.

No less than 250 prisoners in our batch received injuries in the stampede. The Americans, who were similarly dealt with the day before, had 288 casualties. They sailed from Memel in a ship named *Masuren* and had also suffered severe hardships during the voyage. One American dived overboard when he saw Sweden in the distance, to be killed by small arms fire within yards of the ship.

Prior to the intake from Stalag-Luft VI, the only prisoners at Gross Tychow camp were sixty-four American airmen. Their camp leader was Technical Sergeant R. Chapman. With the American presence being increased by 1,800 with Frank Paules as their camp leader, it was only right in the name of democracy that an election be held to decide between Chapman and Paules. Needless to say, Paules was elected, the American Man of Confidence taking ninety-seven per cent of the votes. The result of the election caused problems. The Camp Commandant, *Oberstleutnant* Bombach, refused to recognize Paules as the camp leader. So far as he was concerned it was still Chapman, although in practice, Chapman was no more than a go-between.

Bombach was one of the worst kind of Germans and boasted that he used the Geneva Convention as toilet paper. He made all the rules in Stalag-Luft IV, and if any were broken we would suffer the consequences. His staff could do no wrong when dealing with wayward *Terrorfliegers* and *Luftgangsters*. One American had been shot dead before our arrival, and we realized that this camp was a most unpleasant one, with a bullying commandant being supported by Pickhardt and his trigger-happy bunch of psychopaths – the pick of the Abwehr.

One of the goons' pastimes was to suddenly open up with bursts of machine-gun fire just over our heads as we pounded the circuit.

144

We would run for cover as the bullets ricochetted around the *Lager* and embedded themselves in the bricks and woodwork. The SS and Gestapo now had a greater authority in the running of the prison camps, and our worst fears were that these harassments by the goons were a prelude to a massacre.

We had been in the camp for no longer than a week when we learned of the abortive attempt on Hitler's life in East Prussia. It was encouraging to know that, at least, there were those Germans prepared to try to assassinate their Führer but, so far as von Stauffenberg and his fellow conspirators were concerned, their attempt had come far too late in the war to deserve any sympathy or regret when they were tried and executed in Berlin.

When the camp was finally completed it comprised four *Lagers* and the *Vorlager*. Each *Lager* was built to hold 1,600 *Kriegies* but, before many months passed, the American *Lagers* 'A', 'B' and 'C' each held over 2,000 airmen, while my *Lager*, *Lager* 'D' held 880 British and Commonwealth airmen and 200 Americans.

John Hooley and I decided that we had had enough of one another's company and parted on good terms. He joined the majority of the Canadians in Barrack Block 1. I stayed with my old team and moved into Barrack Block 5 with them. There was John 'Jake' Akehurst, Larry Bone, John Theckston, Fred 'Andy' Anderson and Leslie 'Mitch' Mitchell. Despite the oppressive and terrorizing conduct of Pickhardt and his henchmen, these marvellous people managed to maintain an extraordinary sense of fun and I considered myself privileged to be one of their company.

'Jake' Akehurst was an escaper. He walked away from a Wellington aircraft that had crash-landed after being shot down. After evading capture for some days, he was eventually cornered and taken prisoner. Whilst being taken to Dulag-Luft by train, he floored his escort and jumped from the slow moving carriage. When he was recaptured he was court-martialled by the Germans for striking his escort and sentenced to six months' solitary confinement in a military prison. To be court-martialled by the enemy was unique. After serving his sentence he was transferred to Stalag-Luft VI at Heydekrug and should have joined the other habitual escapers in Barrack Block 12 of 'A' *Lager*. Instead he

145

came into our room in 'K' *Lager*. Jake and I were good friends.

One day we were pounding the circuit when we got a morbid satisfaction in seeing a goon maintenance worker electrocute himself. He was repairing a power cable strung over the outer fence, when we were amazed to see him jack-knifed over the top of the fence with blue flames shooting from his mouth. He was quite dead but nobody cheered. It occurred to us that Richard Pickhardt may have felt like a bit of fun and switched on the power for kicks. How warped our minds were becoming after a few weeks in Stalag-Luft IV.

Since the D-Day landings Bomber Command had switched its attention to railway marshalling yards, bridges and any other means of communication and transportation which would disrupt the movement of troops and armour to the Second Front in Normandy. While this might have been sound strategy, the constant air strikes played merry hell with the consignments of Red Cross parcels, which were unable to be delivered to the POW camps dotted throughout the Reich and occupied territory. The days had gone when a *Kriegie* could expect to be issued with a whole parcel to last him a week and, to make things more difficult, the German contribution to our diet was dwindling – they were also feeling the pinch. We were lucky if we got a cupful of barley, or a few chunks of boiled horsemeat and perhaps a handful of pig potatoes, to last until we knew not when. We were all becoming very emaciated and looking more to self-survival.

The appalling conditions under which we existed in Stalag-Luft IV did not favour good personal hygiene and resulted in the barrack blocks soon becoming infested with lice, mice and a variety of creepy-crawlies. This was nothing new, but it meant many more hours to be spent nit-picking – that single-minded pastime to try to reduce the unwanted parasitic population by squashing them between thumbnails, singeing or drowning. Even the goons were plagued with lice, but they did have the benefit of a stock of delousing powder in the *Vorlager*. When autumn gave way to one of the severest winters on record in Northern Europe, the lice needed our company even more and regardless of

146

how many we managed to exterminate, there would always be survivors to carry on irritating us day and night in the quest for blood.

As at Heydekrug, we regularly watched Luftwaffe aircraft fly over the camp as they plied to and from the Eastern Front. One afternoon two Focke Wulf Fw 190 fighter aircraft flew from the east at an altitude of 1,500 feet, wingtip to wingtip. When almost over the camp, one of them slowly rolled on its back and nose-dived as straight as a plumbline, its engine howling. It looked as though it was about to make a hole in 'D' *Lager* and everyone scattered. Fortunately it missed the camp and buried itself in an adjoining field. We all cheered as black oily smoke mushroomed above the crater. Even the goons were unimpressed by the unusual flying display of one of their pilots. The prisoners cheered.

There was a lot of speculation as to the reason for the pilot's loss of control; the popular theory being that he had been wounded in combat and, while being escorted back to base, he passed out or died above the camp. The dead pilot's wingman circled the crash sight a couple of times and flew off. There was little he could do.

We all became anxious once more when the Germans gloated about a victory they had gained at Arnhem, claiming they had annihilated the British 1st Airborne Division and taken thousands of prisoners. They piled on the agony, knowing that any setback by our troops prosecuting the war through the Low Countries would dampen our spirits. Whilst the Arnhem debacle was a temporary setback, the overall news being broadcast by the BBC and picked up by 'Canary' was encouraging.

News about the Home Front could have been a lot better for the Londoners, with the goons making it known that their V-weapons, the V-1 and V-2, were raining down on the capital and destroying the concentration of reserve troops billeted in Hyde Park, Pimlico and on Wandsworth Common. They were convinced that these terror weapons would change the course of the war and assure them victory. It was as though the goons had taken a crash course on how to demoralize enemy prisoners, with Josef Goebbels and William Joyce as guest speakers. Despite all

147

the setbacks we were satisfied that the Allies were winning the war. We dare not consider defeat.

The news from the Russian Front was more encouraging, and with the Red Army's advance into Poland, we wondered how long it would be before we moved camp again. Russian prisoners were being put into the next *Lager* to ours. They looked a sorry sight, just skin and bone hidden by greatcoats and feet covered with strips of hessian. They had been made to walk for weeks on end from the battle zone, many supporting their wounded comrades. Hundreds died of malnutrition and gangrene. We were powerless to ease their plight.

The goons feared the Russians and patrolled their *Lager* in pairs for safety. On one occasion the Russians were kicking up a row in one of their barrack blocks, pleading for food. As they appeared on the verge of rioting, the goons barred the door of the building and sent in an Alsatian dog to quell the disorder. The noise subsided for a while, but the dog was never seen again; it was eaten raw and its bones thrown out of a window in defiance. From the way they were being treated, there was little doubt in my mind that the Russians would resort to cannibalizm.

Christmas 1944 came and went without a lot to celebrate. Our room band provided a little musical entertainment with such instruments as harmonicas, combs and tin cans. There was little to eat and drink and the jokes, lewd and otherwise, had been heard before time and time again. Cigarettes were rationed and few could be spared to gamble. It was freezing and we were burning anything combustible we could find. Things were pretty miserable really. And, to top it all, the goons were boasting again about their glorious army's counter-offensive in the Ardennes, setting us off worrying again. We prayed that the offensive, later to become known as the Battle of the Bulge, would be contained by the Allies.

The Germans were not so keen to let us know that the Ardennes Offensive had petered out after heavy fighting on both sides. We were delighted to learn that Bomber Command had played its part in bombing the Wehrmacht's supply lines, resulting in von Rundstedt's Panzers being starved of fuel and supplies necessary to maintain the offensive. And neither did the Germans let us know that the Red Army had captured Memel and Tilsit, and were by-passing a besieged Königsberg to threaten Warsaw and Danzig. With the Russian Front only 150 miles to the east and closing fast, we were ordered to prepare to move.

A week into February our compound was ordered to parade with our rucksacks. We stood shivering and stamping our feet in a foot of snow while we were counted and formed into groups. I was dressed in an American GI greatcoat, trousers and boots. Under the greatcoat I wore under-clothing, a shirt, pullover and a padding of torn palliasse casing. A sock covered my head and I was also in possession of a blanket.

The Germans had ceased to patrol the Russian *Lager*, and the poor wretches were running riot and trying to break their way into the *Vorlager* where they hoped to find some food. We did not give tuppence for the chances of the Russians staying alive once all other nationals had been evacuated and were beyond the hearing distance of machine-gun fire. We were convinced that Pickhardt and his murderous crew were not going to let the Russians roam the East Pomeranian countryside at will – they were a liability and would be shot 'whilst trying to escape'.

We were also a liability. But the Red Cross had a record of us, and it would be difficult to explain how thousand of Allied airmen could be shot while trying to escape. Therefore, it was the intention of the *Oberkommando der Wehrmacht* to keep us out of the way of the armies advancing from the east and from the west. Yet, apart from initially heading towards the west, they had no idea where they were taking us. The normal German efficiency and planning was breaking down, and the individuals were becoming increasingly concerned with self-survival.

It had been snowing on and off for some weeks and the countryside was covered in a blanket of snow to the depth of two feet. Leaving the camp, we retraced our way along the lane through the trees to the village of Gross Tychow, although at a more leisurely pace than six months before, and with less fear of being assaulted with a bayonet or rifle butt. There were mixed feelings as we passed the deserted railway station and saw that there were no cattle trucks waiting for us. If we were going to walk any distance, then the opportunity to escape may present itself. Jake Akehurst, Mitch Mitchell and I were excited at the prospect of at last making a bid for freedom. We were not prepared to 'sit it out' and, without having any idea what the future held for us, we decided that rather than walk at least 500 miles towards the Allies still struggling towards Germany from the Low Countries, it would be more expedient and sensible to close the gap between the Russian Army and our column once we managed to escape.

We could not have foreseen when the column set off that it would take eighty-two days to cover the distance, including detours in excess of 450 miles, before it finally reached an army prison camp, Stalag 11B, on Lüneburg Heath. This was later referred to as the notorious 'Hunger March', but, sadly, it was also a death march for many prisoners.

With heads down against freezing winds we trudged on four abreast, the reasoning being that should we come under air attack, two would dive into the snow on one side of the road and two the other. The same drill applied when we halted for ten minutes rest in every hour, when we either sat on our rucksacks or in the snow. Once we sat down, it became harder and harder to get to our feet again. Our footwear was quite inadequate for the conditions we were having to put up with and our feet were soon wet and numb with cold. Spaced every few hundred yards along the length of the column were elderly goons riding on horsedrawn carts. The carts were for the purpose of conveying those wretched POWs who were too ill to continue the march. Although any *Kriegie* would have been extremely grateful for a ride on a cart, we satisfied ourselves that any space available on these carts would be taken up by the genuinely sick who required medical attention. One did not need to be qualified as a doctor to recognize the needy cases. However, as the weeks passed, more and more cartloads of our sick comrades, some beyond all medical aid, would disappear from the columns for some unknown destination. We could only hope that they were taken to hospitals or similar havens to receive proper medical care. Time would show that many simply disappeared and were not heard of again.

The days were endless, and one walked for miles in a kind of stupor, without consciously being aware of surroundings or noticing the now downcast civilians by the roadside.

Where possible we were kept to the byroads as for the most part they were comparatively traffic free. I dogged the footprints of the *Kriegie* in front of me, mesmerized by his snow covered ever-plodding boots. I knew his feet were as leaden as mine, and that we would press on in a zombie-like fashion until we came to a place to stop overnight. There would be a scramble for a piece of floor space and, having staked a claim, we would sink exhaustedly to the ground – unless there was a promise of food, pig swill, raw potatoes, or anything to ease our hunger. We would sleep soundly.

As time passed, to cover a distance of fifteen miles in a day was the exception, with ten miles being the norm. Although it was an effort for the older men, the goons steadfastly kept up with us, although they would take advantage of any room on the carts. Like us, they were also pushed to the limit.

An advance detail of goons, usually with an officer, would visit farms en route to commandeer barns and stables for our overnight accommodation. For a column of prisoners to descend upon a farm would have the same effect as if it had been visited by a plague of locusts, and it was unlikely that the hapless farmer would receive recompense from the military at that stage of the war. Unless everything edible was under lock and key and well away from where we bedded down for the night, it would disappear. As we departed from a farm with our pockets bulging with pilfered dried peas, swedes or potatoes, we had sympathy for the German farmers some of whom, upon seeing our plight, spared as much food as they could to ensure that we got something to eat. One good samaritan slaughtered a lamb and, with a selection of vegetables, made a giant stew for us in a copper in the farmyard. It was rationed out at a cupful each, and he was the farmer of the month. There were many acts of kindness by the people along the route, despite it being an almost impossible task to feed so many starving enemy prisoners.

The goons endeavoured to regulate the marching columns to ensure that they got to a farm an hour or so before dark. This

151

would give them time to count heads and dole out any bread ration before everyone was locked away in a barn or similar building for the night. Bread was the only food the goons gave to us while we were on the march and then we would have to wait days between issues, the equivalent to two or three slices. Everything seemed a problem for the goons.

It was a week after we left Gross Tychow that the Germans miscalculated and it was dark by the time we reached the farm for our overnight stay. We left the road and started down a narrow farm track, which had a hedgerow on one side and deep snow-drifts covering the verges. We still had about 200 yards to go to reach the farm buildings when I noticed a gap in the hedge on the far side of the nearest goon. I only had to look at Jake and Mitch to know that this was our big moment. Checking once more that we were nowhere near a guard, I darted through the gap in the hedge and dived headlong into a snowdrift, at the same time noticing out of the corner of my eye that Jake and Mitch had followed me.

I dared not move until all the column had passed by for fear of presenting a silhouette against the snow for the goons to shoot. As I lay cocooned in the snowdrift I experienced a fear of what would happen to me should I be recaptured and, at the same time, a certain elation that with luck I would soon meet up with the Red Army and be homeward bound.

As I waited for the tail end of the column to make its slow progress past before I dared move, I became aware of the sound of a loud commotion coming from the direction of the farm build-ings; goons were shouting orders and the dogs were barking. Whilst it was not possible for the goons to have taken a head count so soon, I felt that it was unwise to hang around any longer. As quietly as I dared I called into the darkness, repeatedly, fully expecting Jake and Mitch to emerge from nearby snowdrifts. There was no reply, and all had gone quiet at the farm. I felt very much alone.

I got to my feet and began the struggle across a field that seemed to have no other side. The long trek during the previous week had been heavy going, and wading through knee-deep snow was

152

extremely exhausting and soon sapped what energy was left. On one or two occasions I just sank to my knees gasping for breath, and to curse Jake and Mitch for deserting me. (Years later I learned from Jake that they thought I had taken off straight across the field from the column, and they did they their best to catch me up.)

I considered crossing the field to try and pick up their tracks, but felt it wiser to put as much distance as possible between the farm and me. I plodded on.

Eventually reaching a wooded area I found that the going was considerably better; snow was hanging in the branches of the trees rather than laying deep on the trails. I was able to make steady progress and the effort kept me reasonably warm. I was grateful for a period of moonlight now and then, making the surroundings less eerie. I eventually came to a forest glade.

Sawn logs were stacked in neat piles about the clearing, although they were only just discernible in the darkness. Satisfied that I was now well away from the farm and that I was not being pursued by a search party, I was only too ready to lay down to rest my tired limbs.

Brushing the layer of snow off the top of one of the piles of logs, I climbed onto it and stretched out on my back. Lying in state on those logs somewhere in East Pomerania was not the ideal way of spending a night. It was so cold and, whilst I dozed fitfully, it was that freezing temperature that kept me from falling sound asleep. Despite everything, it was still a very exhilarating feeling being free, a feeling that truly compensated for the aching feet and other discomforts. I was confident that I would soon be holding Joyce in my arms once more.

I rested on the logs for about an hour and, refreshed, set forth to meet the Red Army – or perhaps Jake and Mitch.

Chapter 13

FORCE MARCH 400 MILES TO FALLINGSBOSTEL

In a fit of uncontrollable shivering, and teeth chattering like castanets, I eased myself off the logs, to spend a frantic few minutes stamping and slapping to restore circulation to my numb and frozen body. It was a no win situation; I either wore myself out trying to keep warm or I suffered from exposure.

The overcast snow-laden sky completely blotted out the stars and, already disorientated, I set about determining which direction was east. I decided that the sides of the trees bearing the most snow were likely to be facing in an easterly direction. When I left the wooded area behind me, I simply rotated through 360 degrees until the breeze or wind was strongest on my face and hoped I was then facing in an easterly direction.

The night seemed endless and I seemed to trudge for miles deep in thought. I was confident that I was at last on my way home and my imagination ran riot at thoughts of landing in Blighty. When dawn eventually broke, I was delighted to see the first signs of another day were appearing over the horizon directly ahead of me.

Travelling in a wide and snowbound expanse of countryside, I was well away from signs of habitation. There were isolated farm buildings but they were too far away for their occupants, if any, to pose any sort of threat to me. By foraging for food on these farmsteads, I planned to keep pressing on until I made contact with a forward echelon of the Red Army, and I also prayed that it was making better progress than I was.

On one occasion I spotted a column of people in the distance and off to my right. I guessed that they were prisoners moving westwards, possibly a party that had left Stalag-Luft IV after our column.

Before it got dark, I had the good fortune to come upon a potato clamp, and I wasted no time in digging into the mound with my bare hands. After eating my fill, I stuffed my pockets until the extra weight became a problem. Prayers come so readily in adversity, although seldom deemed necessary in more happier circumstances, but I truly thanked the Lord that evening.

During the afternoon, being ready to drop, I crawled under an upturned cart at the edge of a field, and half a mile from what appeared to be farm buildings. Wrapping myself in a blanket and curling up, I was soon sound asleep. I awoke to find it was blowing a blizzard outside, and it was perishing cold. For the next two or three hours, I spent my time alternating between sleep and jogging around the cart to maintain circulation. It was a crazy existence, in which I smoked the last of my cigarettes. Time and time again, I would cock my ear and listen intently for the sound of gunfire, but all was frustratingly quiet. I set off again while it was still light. It was becoming vital that I keep moving for as long as I could, and rest only when I was on the point of collapse.

It was another long and arduous night, made more difficult by having to make detours caused by wide streams and deep snow-drifts. As dawn was breaking, I found that the road on which I was walking led downhill to a hamlet. Rather than repeat the mistake I made in the Moselle Valley after my parachute descent, I turned off the road and started to climb a ridge overlooking the hamlet. I was no more than thirty yards from the road, when the ground gave way beneath my feet and I dropped into a dugout, landing with such a jolt that I bit my tongue.

This mantrap was probably the work of the local Home Guard as a defensive position overlooking the east–west road through the hamlet. While the Home Guard had been disbanded in the UK after the threat of invasion had passed, Hitler had called upon his male pensioners and teenagers to take up rifles and bazookas, and prepare themselves to repel all invaders.

The dugout was four feet deep and thirty inches in diameter. It had been covered with twigs which were hidden under a layer of snow.

It was too great an effort for me to climb out of the dugout just then, and I took a chance that, for the time being, the Home Guard would have no need to inspect or take up their defensive positions. Although rather cramped the dugout was snug and out of the freezing wind.

Some time later I was alerted by the sound of engines ticking over. Cautiously, I popped my head through the branches over my shelter hoping to see red stars on the sides of tanks, but instead of Russian tanks, I saw the black and white crosses clearly visible on the sides of German half-track troop carriers. There were three of them parked along the side of the road, and there was a chorus line of soldiers busy etching patterns in the snow. A small group of officers had their heads together studying what must have been an ordnance map. The engines were kept running for about thirty minutes while the soldiers frolicked in the snow and became involved in a friendly snowball fight, some coming to within yards of my hideout. That was too close for my comfort. They were young and looked like recruits in new uniforms, compared with the battle weary and unkempt veterans I had seen on the troop trains.

It was with great relief that I heard the convoy move off to make its way through the hamlet, accelerating towards the front line that could not be so many miles ahead of them. I guessed that their next battle would be infinitely more deadly than a snowball fight.

The presence of military units in the area boosted my morale and, whether by imagination or not, I convinced myself that I could detect the distant sound of gunfire.

The road leading through the hamlet was a busy one, with military vehicles passing through it in both directions, often in convoy like the troop carriers. The hamlet itself appeared deserted, the inhabitants were either in hibernation or had fled before the Russian advance.

As soon as darkness fell I decided to make a move. I was not prepared for the difficulty I had in trying to extricate myself from the dugout. After squatting all day with my knees under my chin, I had lost all feeling in my lower limbs. As a result of the paralysis, I had to lever myself out with my elbows and this was far from easy in the confined space. After a supreme effort, I managed to ease myself out to lie panting in the snow. It seemed ages before I managed to restore the circulation into my legs and to be able to stand. It was a most anxious time and I had to admit to myself that I would be unable to carry on much longer in my condition.

I had not travelled far before it began to snow again, not heavy, but enough to make visibility poor and the going hard as I skirted the hamlet. I was really in trouble, light-headed, terribly weak and now I had vertigo. After all the effort, I doubted whether I had travelled a total distance of more than ten miles since leaving the column and the Russians had probably halted to consolidate their line of advance.

As I stumbled through the night, barely able to keep on my feet, I began to hallucinate. The first mirage was of a giant stack of Red Cross parcels towering in the snow before me, but it was only a split second before the vision disappeared. The next occasion was when I was about to take a hefty bite out of a handsome luncheon meat sausage, when it, too, vanished. I was really out of sorts and to make things even worse I found myself struggling against a blizzard, which was no mirage.

Suddenly I came upon a hut beside the lane I was following, and hoping to find some shelter I made my way over to it. I was almost on top of the hut, when a voice from within it ordered me to halt and put my hands up. Inside was a sentry fumbling for his rifle, and in a voice that betrayed his panic I was again ordered to halt. As I leaned against the *Posten* box I must have looked like nothing on earth to him and I did not know whether to laugh or cry. So much for that attempt to reach freedom. I wanted to sleep. The Luftwaffe sentry had an impediment in his speech, and insisted that I gave him the password or produced my ID card. I showed him my *Kriegie* dog tags and explained who I was, and that I had

157

somehow become separated from my column. This flustered him, and he almost passed me his rifle to hold but thought better of it as he cranked away at his field telephone to summon assistance. He jabbered away on the telephone, trying to explain to the person on the other end that he had detained a prisoner trying to gain access to the airfield. While were waiting for the escort to arrive, the sentry was almost apologetic at having to detain me and under any other circumstances, I suppose I would have felt sorry for complicating his war.

We were soon joined by a sergeant and an airman. They appeared friendly, but I was left in no doubt that they would not hesitate to use the pistols they were holding if it became necessary. After I had repeated who I was, they showed some concern about my physical condition; they even supported me between them. As we left the Sergeant good-humouredly kidded the cock-a-hoop sentry that he would be recommended for the Iron Cross 1st Class for behaving with total disregard for personal safety in detaining me. We walked for two or three hundred yards to a large country house. Several Junkers Ju52 transport aircraft were dispersed either side of the approach to the house. They were snowbound and anchored to the ground and, from the sort of weather we were having, they looked as though they were going to be grounded for a long time.

My recollection of the events during the following twenty-four hours is vague but, after I had satisfied the Germans that I was a bona fide *Kriegie*, I was given food and facilities to wash and shave in hot water. Next morning I woke up to find myself in a large armchair in a dimly lit cellar crammed with furniture and bric-a-brac. I had no idea how long I had slept, but daylight was shining through the outside grating behind a high window. I felt a lot better in myself, and was so comfortable that I was reluctant to leave the chair; instead, I rearranged the blankets and dozed off again.

I was aroused by the friendly Sergeant holding a tray. On it was my breakfast of two boiled eggs, a piece of bread, and a mug of coffee. With some difficulty we managed to carry out a reasonable conversation. He apologized for locking me in the cellar, adding that it was on his commanding officer's orders as a safety precaution. Officers of higher rank visiting the airstrip and seeing me could insist that Hitler's directive, that escaping POWs should be shot, be complied with. This possibility caused me fresh anxiety, despite the good thinking on the CO's part.

The Sergeant went on to say that I was to be taken to a POW column to continue my journey westward as soon as one could be located. There was a search team out already looking for such a column.

I had wandered on to a temporary airstrip which, flying weather permitting, supplied the Wehrmacht divisions on the Eastern Front with food and equipment. The house had been commandeered by the Luftwaffe, its previous wealthy tenants had only recently been evacuated.

The CO was in a dilemma. He would either have to destroy his aircraft before being overrun by the Red Army, or take a chance and hang on with the hope that weather conditions would improve so that he could fly out.

I was then left alone for a couple of hours, before being visited by the CO. A major, he was at least fifty years of age and wore many decorations. With him were three young pilots. The Major asked me if I was feeling better and observed that, whilst he admired my spirit, to escape in conditions where the temperature had dropped to minus twelve degrees centigrade was to be discouraged. And furthermore, there was no way I could have got one of his aircraft off the ground.

The Sergeant and a corporal joined the gathering and reported that a column of prisoners had been located. The Major wished me luck, and I thanked him for his kindness and consideration with all sincerity.

Once again I had been treated with decency by the true soldiers of the war, and I did not want them to suspect that I was as lousy as a hedgehog. The warmth and comfort of the cellar had reactivated the little blighters and I barely refrained from frantically scratching myself.

After leaving the cellar we passed a comfortable room with a roaring log fire, which I vaguely remembered from the night, or it could have been two nights, before. The Major was standing with his back to the hearth and, with a smile he warned me that if I ventured near his aeroplanes again I would be shot. I believe he meant it.

I sat beside the Sergeant on the back seat of a *Kübelwagen* (Volkswagen Jeep). A corporal drove the car and he had his work cut out negotiating the lanes and road covered with ice and drifting snow. After a mile or so we came to a roadside inn. After parking the runabout behind the premises, my escort took me into a cosy parlour and sat me on a bench beside the fire. We were then joined by two, not unattractive, females who fondly kissed and embraced the airmen. This was a bit too embarrassing for a *Kriegie* who had not been near a woman for nearly two years. Staring into the fire, I warmed my hands and wondered what was going to take place next.

I was introduced to the landladies, and it was explained how I came to be sitting in their parlour. From that moment I was treated like a celebrity by the two ladies. They handed me a stein of beer and were full of admiration for the *Engländer* who had tried to steal one of the Luftwaffe's aircraft. While they were so nice about everything, I made no attempt to disillusion them.

The beer helped wash down a meal of bread and sausage, but I soon began to feel bloated and woozy. The beer was strong. The airmen must have enjoyed an intimate relationship with the charming ladies, and I concluded that the temporary presence of the Luftwaffe at the nearby estate must have brought excitement into the ladies' lives. As I left the inn I was handed a large loaf of bread, and I could not have been more delighted with such generosity. It was only after I had got well away from their premises that I realized that they still had my *Kriegie* ID discs which they looked at out of curiosity. Whether the discs had been kept as souvenirs I could not say, but being abroad in Germany without them could lead to complications.

We motored on for at least thirty miles before we caught up with a column of prisoners. I tucked my loaf out of sight in my blanket, not wishing to share it with complete strangers unless absolutely necessary. After the Sergeant had a word with the goon who appeared to be in charge of the column, I was reprimanded and then allowed to join the end of the column which was made up of about 1,000 Americans who were the last to leave Stalag-Luft IV. They were dubious about my familiarity with the two Germans in the runabout, and who had gone back the way they came, waving goodbye. I explained all, and was soon trading potatoes for Lucky Strike and Camel cigarettes.

It was back to the same routine again. So much for that attempt to reach Uncle Joe's troops.

Being the last column out of the camp, the Americans were finding that the farmers along the way had already given as much food as they could to the other columns, and I realized that I would have to be careful with the few potatoes and bread I had left.

A couple of days after I joined the column we stayed at a farm on the outskirts of Neubrandenburg. We were told that the goons were endeavouring to find out where we should be taken next, and we were issued with half a loaf of bread each.

We resumed the trek westwards, making heavy going of it. My feet hurt terribly, but I dared not take my boots off as I would never get them on again. I had to get used to being a cripple.

Sometime in February, we queued at one farm for a piece of bread. I hid the bread under my blanket and went out scavenging in the farmyard for anything worth eating but, with two or three hundred other prisoners with the same thing in mind, the search proved fruitless. As I entered the barn, I spotted a *Kriegie* hurrying away from my patch of floorspace. I knew instinctively the something was wrong and, on checking under my blanket, saw that my bread ration was missing. I hurried over to where the suspect thief was kneeling, but no words of accusation from me were required. He turned and shamefacedly handed back my bread. The sheer relief of successfully recovering a few ounces of black bread was sufficient to dismiss from my mind any thought of retaliation by physical violence. In any event, I was in no condition to sustain an assault on anyone. Given the opportunity, we would steal food; the only difference in this unfortunate episode was that he had committed the sin of stealing from a fellow *Kriegie* and he would have to live with that. This particular fellow avoided me from then on.

161

During the hourly rest periods we would listen intently, hoping to pick up the sound of gunfire from the easterly direction. We had no idea how the war was progressing as the last news we received was while we were still at Stalag-Luft IV. For all we knew the Allied armies could be only a few miles away although there was no sound of gunfire to confirm this hopeful thinking.

We shambled through, or bypassed, towns with such names as Waren, Parchim and Ludwigslust as the cruel winter turned to spring and we also left cartloads of sick Americans behind.

With the clearer skies, we occasionally witnessed aerial scenes reminiscent of the Battle of Britain, with heavy formations of Flying Fortresses and Liberators of the US 8th Air Force leaving their telltale contrails as they flew on to their targets. Although now protected by the P51 Mustang fighters, the formations were still savaged by the tenacious Luftwaffe fighters. The gallant losers, friend or foe, fell out of the sky in slow motion, with minute white dots or parachutes even more slowly following the heavy metal down.

Starvation and dysentery were now taking their toll in the column. We all looked gaunt and emaciated and even the goons were faring no better. I think we all knew that we could not go on much longer, marching because the Germans did not know where to put us, especially as the Allies were on the offensive in the west. Hitler's army was on the verge of defeat, his airforce overwhelmed, his navy neutralized, and his cities razed to the ground. It was little wonder that some of our escorts looked upon us as objects for retaliation and could still be brutal and heavy-handed. Some of the more prudent goons, sensing that the shoe would soon be on the other foot, became a good deal more considerate towards us in the hope that they would be dealt with more leniently when the day of reckoning finally came.

The Wehrmacht, refugees and other Germans using horsedrawn transport also had their casualties. We passed many bloated carcasses of horses, with their legs rigid, like discarded nursery dobbins. The stench and attendant buzzing insects certainly put us off any thought of cutting out steaks although we would have still relished a bowl of diced horsemeat stew there and then.

At the last barn I stayed at on that march, I found a number of sacks of dried peas. I prised two boards away from the side of the barn near where I was lying. Squeezing myself through the narrow opening, I crept through to a store shed to try the outer door to freedom – I hoped. The door was locked and secured, and any noise trying to force it would have attracted the attention of the sentry, wherever he was. Instead, we had to be content to fill our pockets with dried peas before I replaced the boards. When we moved off next morning many of us waddled down the road like animated beanbags – all pockets and midrifts bulging.

On 28 March we thankfully climbed into cattle trucks at Uelzen railway station. We were squeezed in the trucks until there was standing room only, and in the confined space we reeked like a refuse tip in a heatwave. We were very relieved to learn that it was only a journey of fifty miles to Fallingbostel on the Lüneburg Heath.

From the railway station we walked a mile or so to Stalag IIB POW Camp. It was situated approximately thirty miles due north of Hannover and had been built on wild scrub and woodland; one could understand why the surrounding countryside had been designated a tank and artillery training area. A large camp, it was originally built to confine Allied soldiers, but now the German administration was overwhelmed by the influx of airmen from the east. It now held something like 40,000 starving prisoners.

Within an hour or so of entering the camp I was delighted to meet up with my pals whom I had not seen since I left the column in February. Alan Hamer confirmed that Jake and Mitch had left the column the same time as I made a break for it, and they had not been seen since. We could only conclude that they must have made contact with the Red Army and were free, unless something serious had befallen them. There was not a lot of news to catch up on, and we set about foraging for food in a camp where prisoners were dying of dysentery, battle wounds and despair.

At a distance of just over two miles to the north of Stalag IIB was another camp at Örbke. A few months earlier prisoners were evacuated from Stalag IIB in Thorn, Poland and most travelled by train to a new camp at Örbke. Although it was basically a camp for army POWs and airmen were in the minority, Dixie Deans still kept his authority as the airmen's camp leader.

Stalag IIB smelt of death which was always present from malnutrition, typhus and unattended combat wounds. Stacks of makeshift coffins outside the wire fence would have to be replaced as they were used to bury the dead. At that time the conditions in the camp were just marginally better than at a concentration camp a few miles up the road at Bergen-Belsen.

One slept in the *Lager* where there was a suitable place to lie, and the days were spent chatting with pitifully thin and bewildered men who as guardsmen, paratroopers and glider pilots, had been captured since the D-Day landings, especially at Arnhem and during the Ardennes offensive. I managed to trade a paratrooper's jumping jacket for a handful of dried peas and my greatcoat. Already I was preparing for the next opportunity to escape. We were given very little food by the goons and, despite all my efforts, I was unable to get myself on an army foraging party which left the camp daily to find a potato clamp to obtain some food, whatever it might be.

During my stay at Stalag IIB, I managed to take my boots off to have a look at my feet. They were as I expected them to be, absolutely filthy and anti-social. I stank. I was amazed to find that I no longer had any toe nails, they having come unstuck from my feet and lodged in places which increased my discomfort on the march. Lack of calcium and continual foot-slogging were the suggested causes of toe-nail shedding. Nothing could be done to remedy the problem in the circumstances. It involved considerable effort, not only to get my boots off but also to get them on again after I had managed to get rid of some of the filth. Not being in the peak of condition I puffed and blowed – and swore at the GI issue brown boots.

Like most of the *Kriegies*, I was beginning to take on the appearance of a dirty tramp who never shaved. With hair on head and face growing ever longer, it became increasingly difficult to recognise mates one had not seen for weeks. Hunger was with us all the time and despair.

We were in the camp for ten long days, witnessing death and

164

starvation on a frightening scale, before we were paraded ready for another march away from our advancing troops. The British Second Army was advancing on Osnabrück, no more than eighty miles to the west. It was rumoured that we were bound for the Harz Mountains, a picturesque area a few days march from Fallingbostel due south. Fifty of our colleagues had already been murdered following their escape from Stalag-Luft III, and I had no reason to believe that the Germans, particularly SS Units, would not commit further atrocities against their prisoners, even at this stage of the war. I was far from happy with the way things were turning out.

Chapter 14

DODGING THE ENEMY ON LÜNEBURG HEATH

It was mid-morning on 8 April when we left Stalag IIB and took the road south-east towards Celle. I was by now wearing American GI issue shirt, trousers, boots and a paratrooper's jumping jacket. I was carrying a blanket and a large sock full of dried peas. My hair and beard were long, curly and unkempt and, despite the eight days' rest at the camp, my swollen and blistered feet were still crippling me, although I was certainly not alone in that respect. We ambled out of the main gate and must have looked like a tramps' charity walk, complete with full complement of lice.

Many of the goons had seen active service in both World Wars, and it was noticeable that they were also disenchanted with the prospect of tramping around Germany for a few weeks more. With their Fatherland being invaded from east and west they were naturally concerned for the safety of their loved ones: many would contemplate deserting rather than risk the possibility of becoming prisoners of war themselves and facing charges of war crimes. Some of those who had always shown hostility towards us were suddenly becoming almost charitable, although far too treacherous to be trusted.

After slow progress for the first fifty minutes, the column took its ten minute rest period in a wooded area surrounded by heathland.

We paired off to either side of the road to relax and enjoy the warmth of the sun, or to have a session of nit-picking. The little buggers never let up for one minute. I settled down on the greensward with my mates with our backs to a clump of shrubbery. Behind the shrubbery there was a shallow ditch and plenty of under-growth to provide ideal cover for anyone. I could hardly contain my excitement. Larry Bone was in no physical shape for an escape attempt and the others in my group decided to stay with the column. A chap who was in the next barrack block to mine at Stalag-Luft VI, the poet Reginald Goodenough, whispered that he would come with me. The next few minutes were spent anxiously waiting for the goons to look away from us before it was time to fall in again. They did look away, and as they did so Goodie and I rolled back-wards into the ditch and quietly slid into the undergrowth. Simultaneously, other *Kriegies* closed the gaps we left. We held our breath and prayed that our absence from the column would not be spotted. The following few minutes seemed an eternity until the column was ordered to its feet and resumed its journey.

We decided not to move until it got dark, and retreated deeper into the copse. During the rest of the day column after column of refugees and POWs passed along the road, interspersed with German military units on foot or with light mechanized and horse-drawn transport. The civilian refugees were on foot, except for a few that possessed bicycles or horsedrawn carts. The fear of being strafed by enemy aircraft did tend to loosen the bowels, and the copse was treated as a place of relief by the refugees who provided us with some queer scenes.

It was necessary to wait for darkness before daring to cross the road unseen and head west to meet up with the Allies, and while waiting we got to know one another more. 'Goodie' Goodenough was an RAF Flight Sergeant of 77 Squadron, Bomber Command. He was shot down on a raid to Düsseldorf in June 1942. A Londoner from Clapham Common, he was a married man who, perhaps for a better reason than I, was intent on getting back to his loved ones as soon as he was able. In camp he tended to keep to himself and had what was considered to be a warped sense of humour. He was a poet.

167

Taking stock of our food supplies we found that between us we possessed a dirty sock full of dried peas, a few potatoes, and another sock full of cigarette ends Goodie had collected during his travels. The fact that we had not a match between us caused some consternation, particularly as we could not reckon on how long it would take before we made contact with Monty's warriors before we could hope for a cigarette. We would steadily become more and more disgruntled as the craving for a cigarette grew.

As the day wore on we became aware of some air activity, and on one or two occasions managed to catch a glimpse of low flying RAF Hawker Typhoons sporting the black and white striped identification markings on the underside of their wings. To see our fighters was morale boosting, particularly as they appeared to be able to maraud unchallenged by the Luftwaffe.

Just before nightfall, a caravan of refugees pulled on to the heath just across the road from where we were. They pitched camp and soon had fires blazing away, the scene taking on the appearance of a gypsy encampment. The camp must have held in the region of a hundred people; people who could still manage to sing and laugh aloud.

Some of the children from the camp came across the road to explore the new territory and they ventured deep into the copse. Despite our efforts to keep out of sight, we were seen by two young girls. Luckily, they took only a passing interest, probably assuming that we were yet another couple of German refugees bedded down for the night. We were relieved that we were not further investigated following their return to the camp. We could not chance that we would be treated on a friendly basis by the children's kinsfolk.

As soon as it was dark we left our shelter which had served us so well during the long hours of waiting. The glow from the camp fires, although not bright, made it difficult for us to skirt the area unseen and we did not want to take too long a detour. Crouching, we scampered across the road and then began an Indian style crawl around the camp. Slithering along a shallow ditch with Goodie close behind me, we rounded a bend to find our way blocked by a couple gasping and grunting in the act of sexual intercourse. Both jolly surprised, and certainly embarrassed, we leapt to our feet and edged apologetically around the pair who were experiencing ecstasy and quite oblivious to what was going on about them – their panting and body rhythm not faltering for one moment.

As we moved away the male voiced something unintelligible, perhaps assuming that we were another couple about to shed the trials and tribulations of being war refugees for a few minutes of rapture. We bade them goodnight and made off across the site as though we were a couple of the campers.

We left the camp behind us without further incident, and took to the heathland in the direction of which, if our luck held, we were likely to make contact with the forward echelons of the 2nd Army. Looking back, we were surprised to see how brightly the camp fires burned, a possible target for night-flying aircraft of the 2nd Tactical Air Force.

The encounter with the lovers in the ditch gave us something to whisper about as we made our way through unknown and certainly hostile territory. The sudden experience of witnessing sexual intercourse rekindled all sorts of pleasant erotic thoughts. Sex had been the farthest thing from our minds during the past few months, and it was nice to have an impromptu reminder of what it was all about.

After an hour or so travelling through hostile territory, we found ourselves splashing about ankle deep in marshland. We had for some time been looking ahead at a silvery landscape under a moonlit sky, and we had to make a wide detour to prevent getting too wet underfoot and bogged down in a strange wilderness.

Soon afterwards we came to a fast flowing stream which we had to cross. Our luck held out – at least mine did – because after walking along the bank for a few hundred yards we came upon a wooden footbridge over the stream. The bridge was old and dilapidated, and I noticed that one of the footplanks was missing. Goodie was too intent on verifying our course and trying to pinpoint the Pole Star. He turned to cross the bridge and disappeared through the gap where the plank should have been. Luckily, he landed feet first and the water only came up to his waist. The sight was too much for me, and for the first time in weeks I curled up with laughter. Goodie swore like a stevedore with a heavy crate on his foot, suggesting that I gave him a hand onto the bank instead of laughing like an hysterical hyena and arousing the neighbourhood. It did not improve his frame of mind when I warned him to be careful not to make the sock of cigarette butts he was carrying too soggy.

With my companion soaked to the waist and tetchy, that unfortunate incident put an end to our meandering that night. As soon as we had found some suitable cover in a thicket we decided to bed down for the night. Goodie draped his wet things on surrounding bushes and we snuggled together under my blanket for warmth. We were already exhausted although we had only covered a few miles since leaving the copse. We were soon sound asleep.

We were abruptly awakened the next morning by the roar of low flying aircraft and, in the near distance, panic-stricken shouts of alarm. We had picked a spot to bed down no more than fifty yards from the road, and in broad daylight we were in a surprisingly exposed position. Soldiers and civilians with children were scrambling for cover in the thicket as four Typhoon fighters of the Allied 2nd Tactical Air Force circled and swooped even lower to strafe the road at tree top level with cannon fire and rocket projectiles. It was bedlam. There were screams as people either died or were injured. Trees were dismembered or splintered in at least three places by the TAF marauders and through it all, Goodie was frantically trying to put on his still damp clothing. Fortunately we never came in the direct line of fire, but with splintered wood flying around us we were terrifyingly close.

As the sound of aircraft faded in the distance, there was a curious silence before the chatter of voices could be heard again. Those frightened people who had intruded almost into our hideout left their bolt holes, presumably to assist as much as they could along the road where the most casualties were likely to have occurred. Goodie and I decided against trying to see just how much grief the Typhoon pilots had caused; if we had been found out for what we were, our chances of staying alive at that time would be nil.

170

The thought occurred to us that, because we were so near a road travelled by refugees, we may have walked in a full circle during the night and were back to where we had started. However, we prided ourselves that our basic navigation skills were second to none and quickly dismissed the silly idea.

In view of all the circumstances, we decided to stay where we were for the rest of the day and try and generate some energy to carry us through the night. Traffic was soon on the move again along the road.

As soon as darkness fell we cut off across the heath, keeping well away from the road for as long as we could. The weather remained dry with patchy cloud, and visibility was ideal for two escaped prisoners trying to navigate across Lüneburg Heath in early April. It was dark enough to provide us with cover in an emergency and light enough for us to pick our way forward at our pace without running into, or stumbling over, obstacles on the ground.

As I was still deaf in one ear it was necessary for me to rely on Goodie to pick up any unusual sounds to give us time to take evasive action. On several occasions throughout the night we would dive for cover as, coming towards us out of the darkness was a column of soldiers, usually in single file, and sometimes leading horsedrawn transport. They were definitely on the retreat, a ghost army moving through the night. Their conversation was always subdued as though their enemy was behind every bush ready to ambush them. Invariably it was the clink of a rifle against a gasmask case or helmet that gave them away. On the one occasion that we came upon such a column and it was too late to take evasive action, we simply walked by them until we saw the opportunity to take cover. It was reasonable to suppose that the retreating Wehrmacht had enough on its mind without being concerned about escaped POWs. If they gave us a thought at all it was that we were just flotsam in a country experiencing the onslaught of the Allies, and I suppose that was our salvation. Goodie wore an army greatcoat and I sported my jumping jacket, although we were never near enough for the goons to get a good look at us.

About midnight we were walking along a footpath with a

railway cutting on one side and a sloping bank with pine trees on the other. On the far side of the cutting we could see a heavy concentration of German troops. There were tanks and troop carriers tucked away under cover of trees. Many of the soldiers were sitting around small camp fires. As they were no threat to us, we decided to sit a while to watch them. Suddenly a lone soldier came out of the shadows near one of the fires. He slid down the embankment opposite to us, crossed the railway lines, and then clambered up the embankment on our side. He was only yards from us when he ducked under the fence and, panting and jabbering incoherently to himself, he jogged off down the lane. He was quite deranged, and we guessed that we had witnessed the desertion of another soldier of the Wehrmacht who had come to the end of his tether and was making for home.

After walking most of the night, and taking many rest periods, we came upon a derelict farm cottage nestled in a wooded hollow and beside a cart track. The roof of the building was intact, but the doors and windows had been removed, the doors being replaced with knee high gates. The wooden staircase to the first floor was in disrepair, having only one or two dangerous looking treads. The attic floor had gaping holes in it and the timbers were unsafe for anyone to put their weight on them. The whole of the ground floor was a pen for a flock of sheep, the only extra being a cast iron bath with a tap to provide supply water for the animals. We quenched our thirsts and cleaned up the best we could without soap.

Once dawn broke and it was light enough to see, we tentatively mounted the rickety staircase and found a place to bed down in the attic under the window. With the blanket wrapped around us we were soon sound asleep again.

It was only a few hours later that I was aroused by Goodie. Following his gaze out of the window, I was shocked to see that the yard of the cottage was full of German soldiers. They seemed to be everywhere. They were feeding themselves, feeding their pack horses and some were cleaning their weapons. They were armed to the teeth and showed all the signs of seasoned fighters. They made good use of the tap water. Our concern was that some inquisitive goon might decide to explore the attic, in which case we would be discovered. While they were not the *Waffen SS*, we did not want to get involved with any German unit at this stage of the conflict.

After what seemed an eternity, the army moved out, but not before they killed two sheep and took their carcases with them. Suddenly all was quiet again.

Leaving Goodie in the attic, I went down into the yard and made an unsuccessful search for scraps of food, matches or anything to light a cigarette butt. As I searched I heard the sound of a two-stroke coming along the lane, and looked up to see a moped come into the yard. It was being ridden by a person I instinctively knew was the farmer coming to attend to his sheep. He could not help but see me standing outside his sheep pen.

Trying not to run, I hurried to the rear of the building and climbed the slope into some trees. Trying to allay any suspicion he may have had, I turned and gave him a friendly wave although I suppose a scruff wearing a para's jumping jacket and GI trousers and boots, was bound to look odd to a shepherd on a moped. I prayed that Goodie would lie doggo and not have a coughing fit.

Taking advantage of the trees for cover, I circled the back of the cottage to get a better view and see what was going on. The bicycle engine was ticking over quietly in the yard, just audible to me as I moved through the trees. Within minutes the engine was revved, and the farmer hared out of the yard and made off in the direction from which he had come. What with seeing a weird looking intruder in his yard, and having sheep stolen, he had reason enough to report the matter to the local police or the military authorities.

Goodie had not been discovered but, by the way the farmer had been muttering to himself a few feet below him, it was apparent that he was upset with the loss of the sheep and the state in which the yard had been left.

Even though it was still light, we had to distance ourselves from the cottage as soon as possible, as the farmer might return with a large search party. Fortunately, we were soon making good time through heavily-wooded countryside and we felt reasonably safe.

We had exhausted nearly all the peas and we were on the lookout for anything to eat. The business of escaping was becoming quite stressful, and we were becoming contrary and argumentative. We would sometimes walk miles without a word being spoken. Nevertheless, I had broken my previous record of being 'on the run' for seventy-four hours, and with Goodie conditions were so much better.

We had to bed down just after midnight because we were exhausted and suffering with diarrhoea. We found a suitable place to sleep under some bushes. Before we dropped off to sleep, we heard the unmistakable rumble of artillery fire in the distance. We were getting near our goal.

Chapter 15

Punting on the River Aller

We were disturbed during the night by the sound of aircraft circling the woods before dropping a parachute flare, its fluorescent white light making the countryside like day and casting stark shifting shadows amongst the trees. We quickly dismissed the idea that the Luftwaffe were searching for sheep stealers, and when the aircraft came round again we saw they were a couple of RAF Typhoons. We guessed that the pilots were looking for enemy troop movements and concentrations to strafe, and this activity gave us added confidence that we would soon be meeting up with our troops. As soon as the flare went out the aircraft flew off to seek the enemy somewhere else.

It must have been well after midnight when we set off again, encouraged by the far off sound of gunfire that had not let up since we first heard it a few hours before, and the presence above of the seemingly unchallenged aircraft of the 2nd TAF. After walking along a cart track over open heathland for some time, we came to a gate giving access to a cobblestoned road. As we passed through the gate we came face to face with two German soldiers deep in conversation. They had rifles slung over their shoulders and were wearing tin helmets. We were too near to about turn without causing suspicion, so we strolled past them and in unison wished them a good night. We were walking away from them when one asked who we were and what we were doing there. Over our shoulders we explained that we were Polish labour, and quickened our pace while they thought that one over. As soon as we felt that we were out of sight we dived into the long grass beside the lane. And only just in time. It may have been the para's jumping jacket or it may have been Goodie's khaki army greatcoat. Whatever it was, the Germans felt the need to question us some more and were doubling along the lane to catch us up, their jackboots stomping on the cobblestones. We hugged the ground and dare not breathe as our pursuers hurried by only a few feet away from us.

Giving them time to get well away, we cut off across the land we had just come from to make a detour of the area which could have a large military presence. Within minutes we were again taking evasive action as another flare dropped from an aircraft caught us out in the open. We dived to the ground, cursing the 2nd TAF for spotlighting us at that precise moment. The aircraft circled until the flare spent itself, and then climbed and flew away. Neither the pilot nor the enemy spotted us under the flare before we dived to the ground. We pressed on, stumbling along forest trails, farm tracks and across heathland, making our way with extreme caution through a dangerous and hostile country. Our greatest problem was encountering increasing numbers of foot soldiers through the night, either in retreat or to take up other positions along the front. We came across weapons laying in ruts, some covered with leaves and dirt for camouflage purposes. The weapons were mostly *Panzerfaust* anti-tank projectiles which were similar to the British PIAT, mines and, in some instances, hand grenades. These booby traps were put there to slow down and kill our soldiers but we could not risk moving them for fear of becoming casualties ourselves. We consoled ourselves with the thought that our lads were up to all sorts of enemy dirty tricks and were capable of looking after themselves.

We came to a hamlet perched on high ground and, if it had not been for smoke curling from a couple of chimneys, it gave the impression of being deserted. Now very conscious of booby traps, we decided not to try and enter any of the cottages. I managed to find four eggs in a small henhouse although there was no sign of any poultry. The eggs were stone cold but fresh, suggesting that the house had recently been abandoned. What a luxury cold raw eggs were to two very hungry escapees.

We were ready for sleep long before it got light and, after finding a suitable place in some bushes, we had a scratch and were soon asleep again. We came to in broad daylight to find that, with uncanny accuracy, we had managed to settle down near a busy road. No more than fifty yards away refugees were streaming along the road, with military transport moving in the same direction.

There was no further need to listen intently for the sound of gunfire, as it was now background noise. It sounded no more than a few miles away and coupled with the sound of artillery fire were the sounds of aircraft hedgehopping and strafing. Although the refugees passed along the road in near silence, we knew there would be pandemonium and death further down the road. It would have been no surprise if refugees diving for cover were to flop down beside us to curse the strafing *Luftgangsters*. We would have been as panic-stricken as the refugees. We knew what a terrifying experience it is to be caught up in an air strike – whether 2nd TAF or Luftwaffe, they were equally as dangerous

After the local air activity had quietened down we were off to sleep again, but only to be aroused a short time afterwards by the sound of someone talking loudly nearby. Opening one eye, I saw two German officers standing and looking directly at us lying under the blanket. They were about eight yards away and were obviously discussing us and probably concluding that we were yet another pair of refugees. They wore the uniforms of a Panzer corps and their less than smart appearance suggested that they had been involved in recent combat. I was thankful the blanket covered my camouflaged jacket.

After a few minutes they disappeared from sight. We then heard orders being shouted, to be followed by the sound of many engines being revved up. Peering through the undergrowth, we were appalled to see tanks and other armoured vehicles being manoeuvred into the trees and coming far too close to us for comfort. We had no option but to leap to our feet and hightail it across the heath as fast as we could, not daring to look back to see what was happening. If we had been spotted by anyone, we must have looked an odd couple disappearing across the heath.

We gained the cover of another copse without being challenged and felt comparatively safe. We did not want to get involved with the military, nor be around if our air forces discovered the armoured column tucked away under the trees.

Although I knew that my para's jacket was a liability in enemy held territory, I was loath to dispose of it because the nights were still cold, and in any case I would soon be in territory held by friendly soldiers – I hoped! We hid again until it got dark, making sure that for the time being we were unlikely to be disturbed.

As soon as it was dark we were off again, now heading for an unusually bright sky beyond some high ground in the south-west. As we made our way slowly to the brow of a hill, we had to be careful not to become silhouetted against the backcloth of light; light that appeared to come from giant arc lamps on the other side of the hill. On reaching the brow of the hill, we gazed in wonder at a fantastic panoramic scene – so beautiful and yet awesome.

Below us and no more than a mile away, at the foot of a shallow decline sloping away from us, was the Verden–Nienburg road crossing our field of view. The road had few bends and ran through avenues of trees. There were many isolated buildings along the stretch of road within our view, probably farm buildings and the whole was brilliantly illuminated by the beam of a searchlight directed horizontally along the road. The source of the light was from some buildings a mile or so off to our right. Birds that shone a silvery colour in the beam of the searchlight were flitting from tree to tree, and it looked for all the world like a Disney fantasia. The birds were not only disturbed because their night had been made into day, but also because they were unable to roost amid the unfamiliar sound of a violent battle taking place.

The fighting was the severest over to our left in the direction of Nienburg. Criss-crossing arcs of tracer were accompanied by mortar and cannon fire. Flares were fired to light up the shadows, and one or two buildings were ablaze. There were smaller skirmishes on either side of the road, particularly in the middle distance. From where we were, we had a wonderful observation point. Not only could we see artillery positions firing towards our

178

lines, but we were able to decide which was the safest route to the farm buildings from which the searchlight was being operated. One thing was certain, our lads were encountering fanatical resistance during their stint of night duty. Men were dying while those birds were flying about in their noisy technicoloured surroundings.

To get to the searchlight we would have to negotiate what war correspondents describe as a 'fluid front line' or 'flexible no man's land', but it was down hill all the way. We would have to be extra vigilant as we did not want to become the targets of snipers, regardless of whose side they were on, nor did we want to blunder into an enemy position waiting to engage our lads.

We soon reached flat countryside and came upon our first obstacle. It was the River Aller, a tributary of the River Weser. It was about thirty feet wide and fast flowing and not a bridge in sight. It was a natural obstacle and we supposed that any of its bridges would be guarded. We were in no condition to swim across at that point, but we were prepared to try to wade across if we could find shallow water.

Shells were now flying over in both directions to land out of our view. The 2nd TAF were doing their thing, dropping flares and shooting places up at a reasonably safe distance from us, but we had to be ready to be bathed in light from one of their flares.

We made our way along the river bank for a few hundred yards and lady luck smiled upon us again. Moored to the river bank was a punt. It had no pole and was in need of repair, but we were used to being up the creek without a paddle. Goodie's sense of humour was returning!

As soon as the punt took our weight water began to slop into it, although we were not too concerned about that so long as we crossed the river. The fast flow of the current swept us along, spinning us around while we tried to coordinate our paddling with the palms of our hands. It was far from easy. Eventually, we made the other side and grabbed tufts of grass to provide anchorage while we scrambled out of the punt.

No sooner had we got on the other bank than I made a fool of myself. It was Goodie's turn to have a good laugh at my expense.

I tried to corner what I thought was a cow. Fresh milk from the udder would have gone down a treat. However, when I did manage to get close to it I could see that it was a young bull. My companion, who was watching the caper in silence, thought that I had completely flipped my lid and was a bloody fool for not knowing the difference between a bull and a cow.

Walking away from that bit of nonsense, we soon had to dive for cover at the sound of an engine. An open topped troop carrying halftrack clattered by so close that we could have touched it. A white star was stencilled on its side, and armed soldiers were leaning forward and peering into the night. This was our first sighting of Allied troops, and I had to stifle the impulse to jump to my feet and wave my arms. However, had either of us done that we would have undoubtedly died instantly. The soldiers were fighting a deadly enemy and did not expect to be waved down by Goodenough and Johnson on Lüneburg Heath just after midnight on Friday 13 April 1945. We would have been shot on sight, a policy adopted in such circumstances by units reconnoitering enemy positions. It was necessary for survival.

With the sights and sounds of war all about us, we at last came close to the farmhouse from which the searchlight was being operated. Excitement mounted as we covered the last few hundred yards, until we were able to hear the engine-driven generator for the searchlight. Wary of sentries posted about the farm, and still uncertain who we were going to find occupying the premises, friend or foe, we approached the buildings cautiously from the shadows.

Looking along the length of the searchlight beams, we could see all types of mechanized armour along the mile or so stretch of road and we could vouch for the fact that our lads were having to struggle for every inch of German soil. Artillery fire came from somewhere behind us and the shells whined overhead to explode beyond the farm, obviously trying to get the range to knock out the searchlight. Lüneburg Heath was not a very healthy place to be at that time, but for Goodie and I freedom was just around the corner of a barn.

Chapter 16

CARE AND ATTENTION FROM THE 53RD WELSH DIVISION

We edged nervously round the barn, although any noise we made would have been drowned out by the background noise of battle. The first thing to come into view was a camouflaged low-loader lorry with a searchlight mounted on it and then, in the shadow behind the lamp, we made out two khaki-clad soldiers in sleeveless leather jackets and tin helmets. They were holding Sten guns across their knees and intently watching the progress of the fighting taking place along the road. With cries of delight, Goodie and I hugged each other and performed a silly waltz in the farmyard, with tears of joy streaming down our cheeks. We were brought back to earth by the soldiers shouting to us to stand still and put up our hands. They trained their Sten guns on us until we satisfied them that we were escaped prisoners of war and from that moment on the British army could not do enough for us. We had made contact with a forward element of the 158 Infantry Brigade, 53rd (Welsh) Division, 21st Army Group, of the Second Army which, not long before had captured the town of Verden situated just over a mile north-west of the farm in which we were standing. The farm had been overrun and occupied by the troops the previous evening.

The two soldiers on searchlight duty could not leave their posts, but invited us into the farmhouse to make ourselves comfortable until we were taken to Brigade HQ at Verden in the morning. We could help ourselves to the army food (compo) rations and anything else we could find to make life easier. The farmer and his family were locked in the cellar for the time being, and they should be left alone.

When we entered the farmhouse we could hardly move for soldiers sleeping soundly on every comfortable piece of furniture and on the floor. The kitchen table was stacked with tins of food, both opened and unopened, and there was an awful waste. We dived in and cleared the scraps first and then finished off the pot of cold tea. We just sat stuffing food into our mouths, as expected of starving ex-*Kriegies*. Within half an hour we both had to dash to the toilet to be violently sick. Our stomachs were not used to such good food although the squaddies had a different opinion of their compo rations.

We tried to sleep but it was impossible with the noise outside and we were worrying again about a counter attack and being recaptured.

We investigated the rooms upstairs for something to do. In one room what must have been a valuable collection of cut glass had been smashed to pieces. We took possession of some clean underclothing which we put on as soon as we had cleaned ourselves up. However, the lice soon began to irritate as much as ever.

Just after the break of dawn a Ukrainian farm labourer came into the house and stood grinning at us. He had been living in one of the barns for a number of years, and gave us to understand that he was responsible for much of the damage in the house. To demonstrate his hatred for the Germans, he would go to the cellar door, pound on it and shout abuse at his former masters.

The soldiers, or squaddies, treated us like VIPs. Many sat busily penning letters to their loved ones so that we could post them when we got to Blighty. We were assured that would be far quicker and more reliable than the field post. We were pleased that in some small way we could repay their kindness.

We were promised a first class breakfast. While tea was being brewed, a squaddie chased a chicken across the yard, letting fly at it with a Sten gun. The chicken disintegrated in a cloud of feathers, but he was more successful with another bird. By the use of a flamethrower-cum-barbeque grill we were each given a leg of roast chicken, to be rounded off with cornflakes and evaporated milk, for breakfast. We were sick again.

Shells sounding like express trains still screamed overhead and the ground shook as some exploded quite near. Only Goodie and I appeared concerned about what was going on around us, particularly as it was daylight and the Germans could see what they were aiming at better.

After breakfast we were driven into Verden and, during the short journey, we were amazed at the amount of armour that was passing on its way towards Nienburg. It was a thrill to feel part of it, however non-effective.

We were taken into an inn that had been taken over as a command post, and were introduced to the Major and a captain who looked as though they were modelling the latest fashions in officers' battle fatigues – they were immaculate. We kept our distance. They gave us a short interrogation, and then arranged for a sergeant major to take charge of us. He was to clean us up, kit us out with new uniforms, and then make arrangements for us to get to the 2nd TAF Headquarters at Brussels. Once again I was surprised and delighted at the way we were being looked after at the height of an offensive. It was remarkable.

The Sergeant Major took us straight to another farm which was in the process of being set up as an RAOC depot. The depot was a hive of industry with all sorts of stores being stacked in the barns. Jerrycans filled with petrol were piled high beside the road – a kind of help yourself filling station. It was a very efficient operation, and the squaddies demonstrated that they had had a lot of practice. And the fact that they never ducked or showed any signs of being afraid when shells burst near by, made us believe that the months of combat had made them fatalists.

We were told that they had run into difficulty during the night. A fanatical Nazi paramilitary organization calling themselves 'Werewolves' had put up some stubborn resistance along the road. This had been effectively dealt with and things were on the move again.

The 53rd (Welsh) Division comprised the 4 Welsh, the 71 and

160 Reconnaissance Brigades, and the 158 Infantry Brigade. Since the beginning of the year and the present offensive, the Division had fought their way from Holland into Germany, being involved in the battle of the Reichswald. In the battle of the Reichswald alone, the Division lost half the casualties it had suffered since D-Day. Just over a week before it had captured the town of Osnabrück thirty miles south-west of Verden, such was the pace of the advance against the Wehrmacht desperately defending their Fatherland.

After a short period in which we sat and watched the squaddies doing their thing, and receiving some more hurried letters to post when we got home, the Sergeant Major had organized things in the farmyard. As we stripped off, our clothes were incinerated by a youngster who knew how to handle a flamethrower. We then had a bath in a large trough in the middle of the farmyard, watched by a ring of squaddies to see that the job was done properly. The water was hot thanks to the lad with the flamethrower, and we really went to town with the carbolic soap, scrubbing each other's backs. We were then thoroughly dusted with delousing powder, and it was wonderful to feel really clean once more. A dispatch rider had managed to get us new uniforms and underclothing, but while Goodie had some new boots I had to wear plimsolls because of the condition of my feet. We sat for a while longer until another dispatch rider parked his motorcycle, and took a barber's kit out of a pannier. He was the brigade barber. He gave us a short back and sides, and got rid of our beards with a cut-throat razor. We now looked like two underfed, but happy, rookie soldiers. And we wanted to retreat as far away from the enemy as we could – just in case there was a counter offensive. We tried not to show our concern.

Soon after midday we were on our way home. We were supplied with a jeep, a Sten gun, some rations and an ordnance map of the area. We were given the directions to reach a displaced persons camp set up between Osnabrück and Rheine. At the camp we were to contact a British major who would arrange a flight to Brussels for us the next day. The road was well signposted, and we would be motoring against heavy oncoming traffic. There would be many military policemen controlling traffic en route and they would help us if we got into difficulties. We were given temporary identification papers and a chit to prove we had been properly deloused.

We left the Sergeant Major and the Division to continue their offensive for another three weeks before the war came to an end and we wondered how many would die in battle before our bundles of letters would be delivered.

Not far from Stalag 11B the British 11th Armoured Division had come upon Belsen Concentration Camp. The world was in for a shock. We drove south-west.

Whilst we were able to make good time, we were moving against a tide of tanks, transporters and supply trucks. And all the drivers seemed anxious to reach their destinations. It was a fantastic and unforgettable experience to see the tanks nose to tail and causing some bottlenecks on roads in the villages. As each tank negotiated a corner, its tracks left holes in the road. German civilians and the Pioneer Corps had a full time job of filling in the holes as the tanks made them.

Goodie and I were amazed at the transformation that took place before our eyes as we passed through these villages. As we approached them the buildings looked normal and intact, but as we passed through them and looked back the devastation caused by tanks, artillery and mortar fire, and even air strikes, was appalling. It was hard to believe that we were looking at the same village.

By-passing Osnabrück we arrived at the displaced persons camp during the afternoon. It was a large field with one or two marquees erected in it. It was swarming with people of every race and creed. The Major was the only Englishman in the camp and was delighted to have us join him. He had been placed in charge of the camp a couple of days before and appeared quite out of his depth. Displaced persons camps would be set up in many parts of Germany in the weeks to come, but this unfortunate soldier had been ordered to set up one of the first. It was something he had not been trained for, and he was thoroughly unhappy. We stayed with him in the camp overnight, and next morning he

185

conveyed us the short distance to Rheine airfield for the flight to Brussels.

As the Major had little idea of what was required, Goodie and I were at a loss to help him to any great extent. As long as the weather remained dry, all he really had to worry about was feeding the poor wretches. There were thousands in the camp, and they had already segregated themselves into their various nationalities. There were groups round roaring fires, fires fed by furniture and timber outbuildings looted from houses in the locality. During the evening we witnessed a killing by a frenzied mob of Ukrainians. One of their own kind had been a collaborator who had volunteered to fight for the Germans in the Russian Army of Liberation (POA) but was liberated before he was called to fight. He was stripped and then set about with all sorts of makeshift weapons. The mob dispersed leaving a battered, bruised and blood-covered body on the ground. Not far away the Russians were playing their squeeze boxes and balalaikas and generally celebrating their freedom.

As the Major, Goodie and I passed among them, our hands were shaken and backs slapped by a multi-national labour force that had just been freed from bondage. Many were under the influence of drink, no doubt from looted alcohol or methylated spirits and, as the night wore on, tempers flared and serious fighting broke out in many parts of the camp.

In the absence of any form of policing or other controls at that time, we felt it prudent to remain in the Major's tent overnight. With the excitement we had very little sleep, but with plenty to eat and smoke we were quite content to wait for the dawn and be on our way to the airfield.

While we waited for transport to take us to the airfield next morning, Goodie and I took a short stroll out of the camp into a built-up area. Allied soldiers outnumbered the civilians on the streets and were treated with respect. I spotted a young man wearing a civilian jacket over a *Kriegsmarine* uniform and, recalling the atrocities at Gross Tychow, I crossed over and blocked his path. The look on his face satisfied any thought of revenge I planned. Gone was the look of arrogance, to be replaced

186

by a look of humiliation and abject despair. His fighting days over, he was one of tens of thousands of Hitler's Wehrmacht who had deserted and were making their way home.

We were eventually collected and driven to Rheine airfield. This airfield had been a Luftwaffe *Nachtjagdgeschwader* (night-fighter squadron) before being neutralized by the 2nd TAF and overrun by our armies in March. Many of the nightfighters that had defended the airspace over the Ruhr Valley and had been responsible for many of Bomber Command's losses over the 'Happy Valley' were now burnt out hulks scattered about the airfield.

The flight to Brussels Airport took less than an hour in a Douglas C-47 Dakota, and the pilot flew at such a height that we had a bird's eye view of the devastation inflicted on the towns and villages along the lines of advance by the Allies. The bumper to bumper convey of armour and other vehicles were the arteries feeding the front line troops. Service areas comprising mountains of jerry cans of fuel and NAAFI wagons could be seen along the busier routes.

From the airport we were taken to a large municipal building in the centre of Brussels. The building had formerly been the Belgian HQ of the Gestapo before it became the 2nd TAF HQ in September 1944 following the liberation of Belgium.

During the next two days we were given a thorough medical check up and kitted out with new uniforms complete with badges of rank and aircrew insignia. I was a very happy warrant officer, but it was still necessary to wear plimsolls for a long time. Although my uniform hung on me and I looked like a bean pole, I was happy to learn that there would be no need to go into hospital and, given a lot of love and understanding and gravy dinners, there should be no reason why I should not fully recover from my ordeal in a matter of weeks.

Surprisingly, apart from obtaining my service particulars and the names of the prison camps in which I had been incarcerated, there was no in-depth debriefing. This was possibly because Goodie and I, to be joined by two more escapees, were the first of many to pass through 2nd TAF HQ, and they were not versed in the art of debriefing. Anyway that was our theory, and we were not particularly bothered.

We were given an advance in pay of the equivalent of £5 in Belgian francs. I am not sure whether we spent wisely, but it was a novelty to hold money instead of a few packets of cigarettes. We held out the money in the palms of our hands for the shopkeepers to take the cost of purchases of perfume or whatever else we decided to buy. The shopkeepers were quite generous and gave us the impression that they were allowing good discounts to two members of the forces that had liberated their country a few months before after five years of Nazi occupation.

On Tuesday 17 April 1945, exactly two years to the day I was shot down, in company with Goodie and two other RAF escapees, I flew to RAF Westcott in Buckinghamshire, in a Dakota aircraft. After a day or so at RAF Cosford, during which time I was found fit for flying, I was given some back-dated pay, and sent home on three months' leave. There was no de-briefing. The RAF had no interest then in what happened to our aircraft and, more importantly, its crew. Steve Tomyn, our pilot, was simply a statistic.

A week later Joyce and I were romantically reunited as we embraced under the clock at Kings Cross railway station and, on 8 May we joined the revellers in Trafalgar Square and celebrated the victory in Europe. A few days later we travelled north for me to meet Joyce's family, and after what can only be described as a whirlwind courtship we married at Horden Parish Church, Co Durham, on 19 May 1945.

POSTSCRIPT

The other members of my crew, Bert, Bill and Geoff, who were evacuated to Stalag 357 at Thorn in Poland in July 1944, also suffered considerable hardship before they were liberated by the Allies north of Fallingbostel. Before the camp moved to Örbke on Lüneburg Heath, Bill and many other *Kriegies* suffered chronic dysentery. It was some weeks before Bill was well enough to stand without assistance.

Stalag 357 was on the move again in April when Stalag 11B was being evacuated. Many sick and dying prisoners were left behind as the columns moved slowly north-east in the general direction of Lübeck. Dixie Deans moved between the columns on a commandeered cycle, doing his best to boost morale and get hold of some food. While many were starving to death, Dixie talked the German Commandant, *Oberst* Ossman, into conveying him to the Red Cross Store at Lübeck to try to organize a supply of parcels. He arranged for a convoy of vehicles loaded with parcels to meet the columns in the Gresse area thirty miles south of Lübeck.

While the thousands of *Kriegies* queued to receive a food issue in broad daylight, a number of 2nd TAF Typhoon aircraft strafed the columns. A total of thirty prisoners died instantly from cannon and rocket fire, while a further forty-five were conveyed to hospital suffering from serious wounds. Three of the casualties were later to die from their wounds. It was a time when bewildered *Kriegies* could do no more than watch their comrades die from typhus and starvation and then to make matters worse, to witness

189

'friendly' aircraft slaughter even more of their comrades a few days before liberation by the Allied armies.

Along with those who had not already made a run for it, *Oberst* Ossman surrendered to Dixie Deans before the first Allied scout car made an appearance. Ossman was playing safe; after all, had he not condescended to let Dixie have the use of his Mercedes to make the trip to Lübeck to organize food supplies?

For his selfless devotion to the welfare of his fellow men, Warrant Officer Deans was made a Member of the British Empire. The Citation ends with the words 'He was loved by all'. This extraordinary man passed away in February 1989 at the age of seventy-five years.

After Reg Goodenough and I escaped on 8 April, the column was also to suffer casualties from 'friendly' fire on 21 April – four days after our arrival in the UK. After making a U-turn near Belsen the column headed north-east towards the Baltic port of Rostock. While the prisoners were sheltering overnight in a village hall at Camin, situated about ten miles east of Gresse, the building was attacked by aircraft of the 2nd TAF and set alight. Two prisoners died instantly, one receiving a direct hit in the face with a cannon shell, while many others died from their injuries in hospital. Reg Goodenough and I would have undoubtedly been in the attacked building had we remained with the column and it is a sad fact that Gresse and Camin were only two places where prisoners died because of mistaken identity as the Allied invasion of Germany took its course. For a *Kriegie* to meet such an end after years in captivity was extremely hard to come to terms with.

The infamous Abwehr officer of Stalag-Luft IV, *Hauptmann* Richard Pickhardt, is said to have fallen into the hands of the Red Army in April 1945. A request by the British Government for him to be handed over to face trial by a British War Crimes Tribunal was refused. Nevertheless, it is fairly certain that Pickhardt got his just desserts either by execution or imprisonment for life at the hands of the Russians.

Jake Akehurst and Mitch Mitchell, who dodged the column with me in East Pomerania, survived a week before they had to reluctantly surrender to the Germans because of illness and general debility through exposure to the awful winter weather. Following a short period in a Danzig prison they were transferred to Stalag-Luft I at Barth. The camp was liberated by the Red Army on 1 May, although the Germans had felt it wise to desert their posts a few hours before the arrival of the Russian soldiers. The camp staff had every reason to fear retribution at the hands of the Red Army.

The theory that our aircraft had been shot down by flak gunners rather than by an enemy nightfighter as we left the target has been strengthened by the investigations of a German air historian named Gebhard Aders. He maintains that *Flakabteilungen* – Anti-Aircraft Units – 491 and 492 were protecting the western approaches to Mannheim on the night of the 16–17 April 1943 and claim to have destroyed our aircraft. It has also been established that our aircraft dived into a field on the outskirts of Kirf and burnt itself out. Steve Tomyn's body was discovered lying in the same field. Kirf is a village twenty miles south-west of Trier and close to the Luxembourg border.

After the war the Commonwealth War Graves Commission exhumed Steve's body at Kirf Cemetery and transferred his remains to Rheinberg War Cemetery near Krefeld in the Ruhr – a cemetery with the graves of 3,000 airmen killed during raids by Bomber Command on targets in and around the Ruhr Valley.

*   *   *

Approximately 125,000 British and Commonwealth aircrew served with Bomber Command squadrons and operational training and conversion units during the period 3 September 1939 to 31 May 1945, and of this total sixty-four point one per cent would be killed in action or die while prisoners of war. Eleven point two per cent were killed in flying or ground accidents or battle action and a further eleven point four per cent were wounded in aircraft during operations or in flying or ground accidents in the UK. The balance of thirteen point three per cent were prisoners of war.

191

From its formation on 1 January 1943 to the cessation of hostilities in May 1945, aircraft of 6 Group RCAF, Bomber Command, flew a total of 39,584 sorties over enemy territory with a loss of 784 aircraft. Wellingtons completed 3,287 sorties with a loss of 147; Halifaxes 28,126 sorties with a loss of 508; and Lancasters made 8,171 sorties with a loss of 109 aircraft. With a crew of five in a Wellington and a crew of seven in a Halifax or Lancaster, a total of at least 5,234 would go missing in action from that group alone, with a less than one in five chance of remaining alive.

Just two weeks after details of our aircraft and crew were wiped off the ops board at Croft, 427 Squadron transferred to Leeming airfield near Northallerton for conversion to Halifaxes. It was to share the airfield with 424 (Tiger) Squadron to the end of the war. 427 Squadron was fully operational by the end of May 1943, and it was that month that the Managing Director of the Metro-Goldwyn-Mayer Film Company, Great Britain, visited the airfield to present Wing Commander Burnside with a bronze figure of the MGM lion. There was also a draw to decide the crew who could rejoice in naming their aircraft Lana Turner, one of the glamorous actresses and pin-up girls of the day. One of my many namesakes, Sergeant E. A. Johnson, a most experienced pilot, drew the winning straw.

In September 1943, Wing Commander Burnside relinquished command of the squadron to the first Canadian CO, Wing Commander R. S. Turnball DFM.

The squadron's first operation was during the night of 3–4 January 1943, when it dispatched six Wellingtons to lay mines off the Frisian Islands, but two had to turn back with mechanical troubles. From that time to the end of the war, the squadron carried out a total of 3,312 sorties over enemy territory with a loss of ninety aircraft. There were 550 aircrew casualties, including 415 killed; 121 baled out or crash landed and were taken prisoners of war. A total of fourteen evaded capture or escaped to reach Allied lines.

Indicative of the bravery of the crews was the number of gallantry awards it earned: Two Conspicuous Gallantry Medals, four Distinguished Service Orders, one Air Force Cross, 147 Distinguished Flying Crosses, sixteen Distinguished Flying Medals and eight Mentions in Dispatches.

The Squadron was disbanded in May 1946 and all Canadian personnel returned home. The Squadron was reactivated in 1952 and equipped with North American F-86F Sabre Jet fighter aircraft – to be superseded by Lockheed F-104 Starfighters. It was again disbanded for a period of twelve months in 1970, before becoming operational with Agusta-Bell CH-135 helicopters. The Squadron is based at Petawawa, Ontario.

The floating coal scuttle named *Insterburg* was built in Sweden in 1919 for Russian owners. It fell into German hands during the invasion of Russia in the Second World War and was used to ship coal between the Baltic ports, eventually being attacked and sunk by RAF fighter-bombers in Kiel Bay on 3 May 1945 – just five days before the end of the war in Europe.

Appendix 1

OPERATIONAL AIRCRAFT AND CREW LOSSES TO 6 GROUP (RCAF), BOMBER COMMAND, DURING THE MONTH OF APRIL 1943.

H Halifax   W Wellington

DATES	TARGETS	SQUADRONS 405	408	419	420	424	425	426	427	428	429	TOTALS
		H	H	H	W	W	W	W	W	W	W	
03–04	Essen	2	2					1				5
04–05	Kiel	1	1				1			1		4
06–07	Minelaying	1										1
08–09	Duisburg			1	1		1	1				4
10–11	Frankfurt				1	1				1	1	4
11–12	Minelaying						1					1
14–15	Stuttgart		2	1	2	1	2					8
16–17	Mannheim		4		1			1	1	1	1	9
20–21	Minelaying			1								1
26–27	Duisburg	1			1			1	1		2	6
28–29	Minelaying			1						2		3
TOTALS		5	9	4	6	2	5	4	2	5	4	**46**

Aircrew Casualties

	405	408	419	420	424	425	426	427	428	429	TOTALS
Killed in action	30	50	14	22	5	13	13	2	20	16	185
Prisoners of war	9	13	8	2	5	8	5	4	6	2	62
Evaded capture		1		2					1		4
Otherwise survived					5		5	4		3	17

Appendix 2

BOMBER COMMAND CASUALTY FIGURES FOR THE RAIDS ON MANNHEIM, GERMANY, AND PILSEN, CZECHOSLOVAKIA DURING THE NIGHT OF THE 16–17 APRIL 1943

Squadron	Aircraft	Target	Killed	POW	Evaded	Survived
10	Halifax	Pilsen				8
15	Stirlings(2)	Mannheim	14	1		
35	Halifax	Pilsen	4	1	2	
49	Lancasters(2)	Pilsen	13	1		
50	Lancasters(3)	Pilsen	11	6	1	5
51	Halifaxes(5)	Pilsen	25	7	4	
61	Lancaster	Pilsen	8			
75	Stirlings(3)	Mannheim	14	1		8
76	Halifaxes(4)	Pilsen	25	3		
77	Halifax	Pilsen	4	3		
78	Halifaxes(2)	Pilsen	3	11		
83	Lancasters(2)	Pilsen	8	6		
90	Stirling	Mannheim		1	7	
100	Lancasters(2)	Pilsen	14			
101	Lancaster	Pilsen	6	1		
102	Halifax	Pilsen	1	2	4	
103	Lancaster	Pilsen	5	2		
156	Lancasters(2)	Pilsen	14			
158	Halifaxes(2)	Pilsen	2	8	4	
166	Wellington	Mannheim	2			3
196	Wellingtons(2)	Mannheim	5			5
214	Stirling	Mannheim	1	3	3	
218	Stirling	Mannheim	5		2	
408	Halifaxes(4)	Pilsen	29			
420	Wellington	Mannheim	4	1		

			A	B	C	D
425	Wellington	Mannheim	2	3		
426	Wellington	Mannheim	5			
427	Wellingtons(2)	Mannheim	1*	4*		5
429	Wellington	Mannheim	4		1	
431	Wellington	Mannheim	1	4		
460	Lancasters(3)	Pilsen	22			
466	Wellington	Mannheim	5			
467	Lancasters(2)	Pilsen	11	3		
TOTALS	59		268	72	28	34

(i) Although the normal crew of a Halifax, Lancaster or Stirling is seven, and five for a Wellington, frequently one or two extra aircrew (or news media observers) were carried for battle experience.

(ii) The 'survivors' either ditched in the sea off the English coast, baled out over, or crash-landed on, friendly soil following damage by enemy action. Many were injured, one fatally.

(iii) * Denotes the author's crew in Wellington X, HE745, Squadron Marking ZL-E.

Source Public Record Office, Kew

Appendix 4

THE BATTLE ORDER OF 6 GROUP (RCAF) BOMBER COMMAND IN APRIL 1943

SQUADRON	CODE NAME	LETTERS	AIRFIELD	AIRCRAFT
405	Vancouver	LQ	Leeming	Halifaxes
408	Goose	EQ	Leeming	Halifaxes
419	Moose	VR	Middleton-St-George	Halifaxes
420	Snowy Owl	PT	Middleton-St-George	Wellingtons
424	Tiger	QB	Topcliffe	Wellingtons
425	Alouette	KW	Dishforth	Wellingtons
426	Thunderbird	OW	Dishforth	Wellingtons
427	Lion	ZL	Croft	Wellingtons
428	Ghost	NA	Dalton	Wellingtons
429	Bison	AL	East Moor	Wellingtons

NOTE: Middleton-St-George (now Teeside Airport) was situated in Country Durham, while all the other airfields were in Yorkshire.